INSIDE BUCHMANISM

INSIDE
BUCHMANISM

*An independent inquiry
into the Oxford Group Movement
and Moral Re-Armament*

BY

GEOFFREY WILLIAMSON

PHILOSOPHICAL LIBRARY
NEW YORK

PUBLISHED, 1955, BY PHILOSOPHICAL LIBRARY, INC.
15 EAST 40TH STREET, NEW YORK 16, N.Y.

PRINTED IN GREAT BRITAIN FOR PHILOSOPHICAL LIBRARY
BY RICHARD CLAY AND COMPANY LTD., BUNGAY, SUFFOLK

Contents

List of Illustrations

Author's Foreword

MY commission to conduct a personal investigation into the activities of the Buchmanites arose in this way. While snatching a brief holiday in Switzerland in July 1949 I passed through Caux, where the founder of the movement, Dr Frank Nathan Daniel Buchman, was presiding over a World Assembly. Though I could not then pause and probe, I saw many things which whetted my curiosity.

Mountain House, the headquarters, was packed with delegates from all over the world—diplomats, politicians, trades union officials, teachers, and students. Fifty-two nations were already represented, it was claimed, and hundreds of other delegates were expected.

I was puzzled to know what magnet was drawing so many contrasting representatives from different countries, classes, and creeds to a mountain spur in Switzerland.

Whatever it was, it had been powerful enough to move the United States House of Representatives to send a bi-partisan delegation to Caux by military plane. The Dutch Cabinet had sent its Minister for Social Affairs, Dr Joekes; Japan had sent its first post-war Premier, Mr Tetsu Katayama; the Speaker of the Ceylon Parliament, Sir F. Molamure, had been there; so had Dr Max Huber, Hon President of the International Red Cross and former President of the International Court, The Hague; so had Dr Frederic Geissbuehler, Secretary of the Swiss Federal Assembly.

Then, in Lausanne, I found that followers of Dr Buchman were hard at work producing a full-length film, scheduled for world-wide distribution. Technicians of repute had come all the way from Hollywood to help and were giving their services free. It was to be an ambitious production, a musical revue expounding the ideology of Moral Re-Armament.

All this I reported to the Editor of a million-sale weekly immediately I got back to London, showing him the printed matter I'd been able to gather in passing.

" It's interesting," he commented. " But what's behind it all? What, exactly, are they supposed to be doing? "

I had to confess that I didn't know. I had a general idea that the Buchmanites were working for unity between nations, though they also seemed to be anti-Communist. Whatever their full purpose, I'd seen enough to realize that they were making a determined, all-out, world-wide drive. It was also apparent that they had very substantial resources behind them, plus the goodwill of countless influential people.

We pondered the problem from every angle, recalling all we had read about Buchmanites in the past. We knew there had been a tendency to belittle them; they had been called " A Salvation Army in Dress Clothes." Sir Alan Herbert had raised objections to their calling themselves " The Oxford Group." There had been questions in Parliament, too, about their efforts to keep their key-workers out of the Services during the war.

At times, we remembered, there had been hints that the whole thing was a " front " for something sinister; some people had declared that it was the tool of Big Business; it had also been dubbed " Pro-Nazi."

But with all this there was nothing concrete to go upon. After some discussion we had to admit that we couldn't honestly determine whether Buchmanism was a good thing or a bad thing. There seemed to be no tangible evidence either way.

It was fairly common knowledge that the members claimed to be " God-controlled "; that they were in the habit of "listening to God" each morning to gain "guidance" for their day's actions. And it was known vaguely that they practised something called "personal evangelism" and talked a lot of jargon about "changing human nature and remaking the world." But how they proposed to achieve these ends we had no idea.

To judge from the press cuttings in two libraries to which I had access nobody else had any idea, either.

For some mysterious reason the vast Assembly at Caux had been all but ignored by the newspapers, though it had been running since the beginning of June. Yet the evidence of my own eyes had told me that something big was brewing there.

Buchmanism, which I, in common with most folk, had long regarded as an obscure, slightly tainted "new religion," was obviously spreading its wings in truly amazing fashion. Almost overnight, or so it seemed to me, it had burgeoned into a powerful world force with limitless implications.

Listening to my story, the Editor's curiosity grew as mine had grown. "So far as I know," I said, "no one has ever taken the trouble to find out the truth about Buchmanism—what it really stands for, how it is run, who runs it, where the money comes from, and so on. Why not let me try?"

It was agreed, finally, that the proposition should be discussed at the next editorial conference, and two days later an envelope marked "personal" was dropped upon my desk. It held a fragment of torn proof with a succinct message typewritten upon the back: "*Yes: everyone is looking forward to your Report on Buchmanism.*"

It was a busy Editor's way of telling me to go ahead, which meant that I was free to tackle the assignment in my own way. I wished for nothing better.

CHAPTER I

Special Plane to Geneva

FROM my place in the queue I could see that the Immigration Officer at Northolt Airport was looking baffled. Wrinkles of perplexity had appeared in his forehead, and as he subjected each successive passport to examination his eyebrows seemed to rise a little higher. At last my own turn came and, noting my profession, he appealed to me in an undertone for enlightenment.

" What's this little lot? " he queried, with an accompanying shrug of the shoulders.

" Special-charter flight to Geneva, Oxford Group," I told him.

" Oh, that's it! " he exclaimed with something like a sigh of relief. " Thanks."

I filed through to the waiting-room, now rapidly filling with passengers—normal travellers as well as those of my own party. There was no one that I knew, but on boarding the coach which had brought us to the airport from the Oxford Group's headquarters in Berkeley Square I had been introduced to a Mr Thomas Powell. He signalled to me now from beside the refreshment bar and invited me to have a cup of coffee with him. Like myself, he knew no one else in the party; like myself, he was a guest of the Group. They had been pressing him to visit Caux for a long time, he intimated.

" I thought about it a good deal," he said; " I refused them last year, but this year I decided I might as well go and see what it's like for myself. I'm going with an open mind."

" Same here," I told him. " I shall be very interested

to hear how it strikes you, and what conclusions you reach."

" You know the place? "

" Hardly. I ' looked in ' last month for an afternoon when I was in Switzerland, on holiday with my family."

" And what did you think of it? "

" I was interested; but by no means convinced. That's why I'm going out again. I want to see more. I want to find out what really is behind it all."

While we were chatting, several batches of passengers were called to the tarmac as different flights left. We'd been scheduled to take off at 3.45, but it was 4.15 before an air hostess appeared to shepherd us to our plane, a gleaming blue Dakota.

Powell paused to admire a towering S.A.S. airliner which had just taxied in, but my gaze had been captured by the name of our own craft. It was called *Maid Marian*, and I took that as a good omen, for one of my recent assignments had taken me to Sherwood Forest, tracing " authentic " haunts of Robin Hood. *Illustrated* had commissioned an article to tie-in with the Quincentenary celebrations at Nottingham. It had been fun. I had even run across the church where Robin and Marian were reputed to have been wed! So I was glad to see Maid Marian's name upon the plane that was to bear me upon a very sharply contrasting assignment. It was one of those quirks, meaningless in themselves, which somehow force their way into the pattern of life.

It was another coincidence that, though we boarded the plane separately as our names were called, I found myself in the seat next to Powell. He was as surprised as I was, and we took up the threads of the conversation we had dropped in the waiting-room.

" How did you first run across the Group? " I asked,

shortly after taking off, when we were battling our way a trifle bumpily across London.

" It was after I'd led a dock strike," he said with a grin. " Two of their people kept calling at my home. I was always ' out ' when they called, but they still kept coming. At last my wife said: ' You'll have to see them,' so I thought I'd hear what they had to say. They talked a lot, and they left me some of their literature. I'm bound to say they seemed very decent chaps, though I didn't really go into things very deeply."

He fell silent for a time after that and busied himself in writing. I assumed that he intended to record his impressions of the trip for the benefit of his friends at home. We were flying smoothly now; at 7,500 feet, said the hostess, as she passed down the aisle with a bulletin from the radio operator. Through the window I looked out across an undulating cloudscape. We were in the clear upper air and the fleecy crests below were agleam. Powell went on plying his pencil, and I withdrew into my thoughts.

I knew now why that Immigration Officer had looked so perplexed. Our plane's complement included a General, a Major, one or two ladies of title, a doctor, an ex-diplomat from Czechoslovakia, some business-men, and two youngsters from Siam. No wonder he had thought us a mixed " little lot."

Yet *Maid Marian* was only one of three special planes chartered to ferry equally " mixed " batches of passengers between Northolt and Geneva, en route for Mountain House, Caux, scene of the Oxford Group's World Assembly for Moral Re-Armament. Other planes were also converging upon Caux from much more distant parts; some from China and Japan; some from America— all bearing delegates of varying race and creed to attend a special session " arranged at the request of leaders of

industry, labour, politics and the professions from the
fifty-nine countries already represented."

*   *   *

I took out my invitation card and studied it thoughtfully.

> Critical world events face all leaders in the immediate weeks
> ahead.   This special Assembly will be an unrivalled opportunity
> to create and strengthen the ideological links between nations
> upon which the unity of Europe and the future of civilization
> depends.

On the reverse side of this card was printed a message
from Hon Prince H. Preston, Jr, Chairman of the bi-
partisan delegation appointed by unanimous consent of
the United States House of Representatives, which visited
Caux, June 1949.

> Now that I have made the preliminary report to the House
> of Representatives I feel at liberty to tell you officially of my
> reaction to the Conference at Caux.
> In the forty years I have been privileged to enjoy life I have
> observed human nature in its many aspects and endeavours.
> Never before have I seen it so thoroughly dedicated to improve-
> ment in the field of human relations.   That you are accomplish-
> ing great good throughout the world is an established fact and
> the great unmatched ideology you offer to a frustrated world is
> undoubtedly the Gibraltar of hope to which we all must cling.

Well, nothing could be more forthright than that,
I thought. Reading that message enhanced my enthusiasm for my own mission; though I decided in the
same flash that I must not allow myself to be influenced
by other people's opinions if I was to live up to my pledge
and keep my investigation absolutely impartial.   I should
have to examine and sift cross-sections of opinion, of
course, but I must not let myself be prejudiced one way or
the other.   I must see everything for myself; gather my
own facts; gain my own impressions, or my whole
mission would prove futile.   If I were going to accept
second-hand opinions I might just as well have stayed in

London to write my report on the strength of the documents and correspondence that were already choking one of the drawers in my filing cabinet.

For I had done a certain amount of research, and data was accumulating so rapidly that the magnitude of the task I had set myself seemed overwhelming. I was, in effect, a one-man fact-finding committee. And I meant to stick to facts.

I had made this resolution clear to members of the Oxford Group I had met in London when making my initial approach. They said they welcomed it; had often wished that some independent publicist would take the trouble to appraise their work seriously.

I was invited to tea so that the terms of my inquiry could be discussed. On that first occasion I was asked to go to a house in Charles Street, Mayfair, where it seemed about twenty Groupists were living a communal life, the premises being placed at their disposal by a supporter who was abroad.

My appointment had been with Garth Lean, a member of the Council of Management, but two of his colleagues were also there to receive me: Captain Rex Dilly, Director of Publications, and W. J. Page, a press officer. I did not know then what I learned later: that Groupists seldom act alone.

I am not playing tricks with time and space, but simply giving you a review of some of the thoughts that were running through my mind as the Dakota bore us across France. Fortified by a snack—cheese salad and a cup of tea—brought to us on a tray by the tireless air hostess, Powell and I lolled back in our yielding, arm-chair seats, and, as he resumed his scribbling, I thought back to that first encounter with the Buchmanites in Charles Street.

To break the tension I decided to place all my cards on the table. I told them I wanted to do justice to my subject and was in no hurry to publish anything. I assured them further that I was prepared to undertake any necessary reading or study to ensure that no phase of the Group's activities was missed. I promised to go to any amount of trouble to ensure scrupulous fairness and 100 per cent accuracy. By such means I hoped to make my ultimate report the most authentic and the most balanced survey of Moral Re-Armament yet attempted by an independent observer. I warned them that this did not mean I should not be critical. They agreed that I would be free to comment as I pleased.

I explained how the brief glimpse I had had of Caux a few weeks before had stimulated my curiosity, and how the visit I had paid to Lausanne to inspect the Group's film-making effort had enhanced that curiosity. Finally, I said I wanted to forget anything I had read about the Group to date and to start building up my own picture of its work.

It sounds a trifle pompous, set down like this, but my three hosts made it clear that they appreciated this candour.

I'd prepared a few questions, and Garth Lean, acting as spokesman, invited me to " fire away." I wanted to know which establishment ranked as Head Office: Hays Mews, London, Mountain House, Caux, or a place I believed they had in Los Angeles. Lean explained that they worked independently, yet always combined resources for any big drive. All would be more or less equally represented; no one would presume to dictate to the other.

Next I asked if it was true that the officials drew no salary. That was perfectly correct, said Lean, adding that certain expenses were allowed, subject to approval by the Finance Committee. He'd mentioned earlier in the interview that he'd just spent a week-end at Caux, so I asked

Mae West, famous Hollywood film star and a convert to Moral Re-Armament, with Dr Buchman in her Hollywood apartment.

Mountain House, Caux, Switzerland, former luxury hotel, now European Headquarters for Moral Re-Armament.

whether that had come under the heading of " expenses."
He told me without rancour that he'd paid everything
himself.

I was puzzled to know how full-time officials found it
possible to carry on without money, especially as they
quite obviously lived on a lavish scale. Even living in a
borrowed house, as they were doing, could not eradicate
the need for cash.

" Perhaps you'll understand better if I cite my own case
as an example," cut in Page. " I was in a job in Northern
Ireland, but I felt a call to devote my whole time to the
work of Moral Re-Armament, so I resigned. I had some
savings, and by surrendering my Life policy I was able
to carry on for a time. Then an old friend in Ireland, who
is also interested in the work, and who had fully approved
my action, undertook to help me in order that I could
keep on with it. He sends me gifts from time to time.
There have been occasions, I admit, when it seemed touch
and go and I wondered how I was going to get along; but
something has always turned up. You'd be surprised."

I didn't press that point at this stage, but asked Lean
whether the Group dispensed any charity. He said no.

I said I'd noticed that Groupists didn't smoke or touch
alcohol, and that women members did not use cosmetics.
Was there any special reason?

" There's no reason; and there are no rules on the
subject," answered Lean. " No one tells anybody not
to smoke. They find they can do without smoking and
without alcohol. It is entirely a personal matter. And,
by the way, you ought to understand that we have no
membership. There's no such thing as enrolling, or
signing on, or taking any pledge or anything. Dr Buchman has always stressed that this is not an organization,
but an organism."

" I see," I replied. " That's really creeping up to

B

another question I have here.   I was just about to ask you where I could find the best summary of the aims, objects, policy, or creed of the Oxford Group—or of Moral Re-Armament, whichever you prefer."

"We are registered as The Oxford Group," said Lean. " An association not for profit.   But look here, if you really want to go into things thoroughly, don't you think it would be best if I were to get you out a dossier? "

" That would be splendid, if you could," I answered. " I'm anxious to grasp all the essentials."

" Right," said Lean.   " It shall be done.   Let's see. Today's Thursday.   Give me till after the week-end. The dossier will be in your hands on Monday morning."

When Monday morning came and there was no dossier I was puzzled.   This feeling grew as the day wore on. And when Tuesday morning came and there was still no dossier on my desk I was prepared to chalk up the first black mark against the Oxford Group.   But suddenly a visitor was announced, and in strode Page, bearing a most formidable package under his arm.

" Garth Lean sends his apologies and hopes you'll forgive him," he said.   " But the job took longer than he'd expected, and he wanted you to have a complete dossier before you."

And complete it seemed, consisting of the following items:

1. A copy of the American edition of Dr Buchman's book, *Remaking the World*.
2. A pamphlet, *The Oxford Group*, by J. P. Thornton-Duesbery, MA, Principal of Wycliffe Hall, Oxford.
3. A book, *That Man Frank Buchman*, by Peter Howard.
4. A Caux Information Service leaflet No. 9 dealing with finances.
5. A copy of *New World News* with more facts on finance.
6. Another book by Peter Howard: *Innocent Men*.
7. A report on the Group's work in South Wales.
8. A survey of an ideological training course for Birmingham shop stewards.

9. A report on the presentation of a Moral Re-Armament play, *The Forgotten Factor*, in the Midlands.
10. The programme for the National Miners' Rally called by Midlands miners' leaders.
11. A brochure *Coal, Key to Recovery*, produced at the request of the Appropriations Committee of the United States Senate.
12. A report on some months' work in German industrial centres, and—for make-weight—two bound volumes of *New World News*.

I was busy with various other journalistic assignments at that time, but I set to work as systematically as I could to digest this formidable array of facts and figures. To do justice to Lean, I must say that he had done a lot to lighten my burden. His letter, accompanying the " exhibits," ran to four pages of single-spaced typing and served to signpost everything for me, lucidly and helpfully. And he concluded by saying:

> We do very much appreciate the thorough way in which you are going into the whole subject, and want to assure you again that we will do everything we can to make any information available that you may wish to have.

For the ensuing fortnight I gave every moment I could to studying that dossier. Besides dipping into it at odd intervals when in my office, I took it home with me for more prolonged study. My family seemed a bit surprised at my taste in literature, but made no comment.

A lot of what I read interested me intensely; a lot I found boring. I was impatient with the repeated use of Moral Re-Armament jargon—a kind of sloganese—and my head used to ring with phrases like: " over-arching ideology," " the uniting ideology of inspired democracy," " the full dimension of change," and so on. It seemed a farrago of nonsense.

But I persevered and, arising out of my studies, I compiled a list of twenty-eight questions touching on points on which I desired enlightenment. Then I telephoned the Buchmanites, who invited me to bring along my list of queries on the following afternoon, August 30.

This time a committee of five awaited me. In addition to Lean, Dilly, and Page, I was now introduced to the Group's secretary, Roland W. Wilson, and to William Yates, National Union of Mineworkers' Branch President at the Victoria Pit, North Staffordshire.

" If it will convince you of my sincerity," declared Yates, without ceremony, " I'll walk all the way back to Stoke! "

He'd come to London for a special broadcast, and someone had reminded him that he mustn't miss his train.

Of course, I hastened to assure him that I did not doubt anyone's sincerity at the moment. And I asked him to believe that I was equally sincere in my endeavour to grasp the full significance of Moral Re-Armament. That was why I had now come along with my list of questions. I wanted facts before trying to form opinions.

As at the first interview, Lean took the chair and we went over my queries one by one. Most of them were answered forthwith, and only occasionally Lean turned to his colleagues to make sure he had their concurrence.

But some of the questions, he said emphatically, could be answered much more satisfactorily at Caux. Three special planes were being made available very soon to take delegates to the Assembly. There would be seats for me— and for my wife, also, if she cared to go.

This sudden invitation came as a complete surprise.

I decided to hedge.

" I'm afraid the decision must rest with my editor," I told them. " As I am expected to make an impartial report, he may not allow me to accept hospitality to that extent."

" Ah," said Lean, hastily. " Perhaps I ought to be more explicit. You would not be under the slightest obligation to the Oxford Group. The invitation has come from Sir Roy Pinsent, who is chartering the planes, and whose guests you and your wife would be. So, you see, your hands would not be tied in any degree. You would be able to carry on your inquiries at Caux as impartially as you please."

" That puts a different complexion on it, certainly," I conceded. " I'll speak to my editor tomorrow and let you know his decision without delay."

" And your wife," said Lean. " Don't forget your wife. There'll be two seats reserved for you, so do try to come. If your paper doesn't feel interested, then come as a private individual. You'll be very welcome."

I talked over this offer with my wife, Margaret, that night, and though the idea of a free trip to Switzerland—a country we both love—held great attraction, she was adamant that it would not be right for her to go. I was engaged upon a serious business assignment, and it might be unwise to turn it into a social jollification. I saw that Margaret was right, though I was sorry for her sake that she had to be left behind.

Next day the editor agreed to my acceptance of Sir Roy Pinsent's offer. And that is how I came to be aboard *Maid Marian*, soaring through the clouds towards Geneva, with my strike-leader acquaintance scribbling away at my side. To this day I have never met my " host," Sir Roy Pinsent, who is, I understand, a prominent industrial solicitor in Birmingham, and an ardent supporter of the Oxford Group. Nor have I been able to decide why he should have gone out of his way to help me in my investigations.

*   *   *

We touched down at Cointrin Airport shortly after 7 p.m. Dusk was deepening into night as we taxied in, but some of our Buchmanite passengers were able to identify fellow Groupists who clustered at the rails, ready to greet them.

Getting through the Customs was a speedy business, and we were soon clambering aboard a sleek, streamlined coach that was waiting to bear us on the last lap of our journey. I lost sight of Powell momentarily, but saved a seat for him next to mine, so when he presently clambered aboard we were able to resume our chat.

Soon we were skimming through the outskirts of Geneva, with a glimpse of the impressive white mass of the Palace of the League of Nations, wraith-like in the night, and a haunting reminder of lost ideals. Was Caux likely to be more blest than Geneva, I wondered?

We had a fifty-mile drive before us, for the most part following the lakeside road, through Versoix, Nyon, Morges, and Lausanne. As our coach sped through the night we turned our attention to picnic packs which had been distributed to us. And to wash down a welcome repast of ham rolls, cheese, biscuits, and fruit, we had non-alcoholic apple-juice, which we drank from cartons.

Bright lights flashed past, with the recurrent roar of oncoming traffic. The coach seemed, in the darkness, to touch incredible speeds. On, on we sped. Lausanne was left behind, then Vevey with its seemingly boundless square and stage-setting streets. Then Montreux, and we gained our first glimpse of Mountain House, high above us in the distance, its lights ablaze. Our coach swung into the mountain road and we now climbed steeply, the powerful engine labouring stubbornly against the increasing gradient. The road narrowed and soon we were swinging round hairpin bends which made most passengers gasp aloud. In some cases the margin of clearance was so slight that it seemed impossible for a coach of such dimensions to negotiate the bend. But our driver, with sure mastery, had a miraculous knack of pivoting his mighty vehicle round with a deft spin of the wheel. The sensation towards the rear of the coach was of being flicked round on the end of a whip-lash.

Glion was reached, and still we climbed, the hairpin bends becoming more numerous. The engine snorted protests, yet proved unflagging. Now, looking downward through the pine trees, we beheld the limitless panorama of Montreux, Clarens, and Vevey far, far below us, with the winding lakeside promenades and the shimmering surface of the lake itself.

" It's marvellous! " commented Powell; as indeed it was.

For once, I thought, the reality lives up to the travel-brochure fantasy: a silhouette whose masses were deep blues and purples, studded with glittering gems.

And then a cry went up:

" Here we are! Here's Mountain House! "

The last bend was negotiated and the coach, gaining level ground, drew up before the bright portals of Mountain House, gliding to a stop with something like a sigh of deep relief from the boiling engine. But that sigh was quickly lost in a welcoming cheer from scores of Buchmanites who came flocking on to the steps to greet our arrival.

I had barely alighted before Garth Lean came shouldering his way towards me.

" Hello! " he cried, his good-natured features lighting up with a smile. " So glad you've come. Had a good journey? Was the flight comfortable? "

He led me through the vestibule to the reception office, and after I had signed the register to comply with tourist regulations, he grabbed my bag and, linking arms, steered me through what seemed a labyrinth of passages towards the stairs.

Surprise number one was that we went down instead of up.

" I suppose you know," explained Lean, " that the entrance hall is on the fourth floor? All the rooms are below stairs. We've got to go to the bottom, I'm afraid, and the lift's not working."

No; I hadn't known about the unusual construction of the place. My visit in July had been so fleeting that I had been unable to take in such details.

" We're sharing a room, if you can stand it," Lean continued as we went down and down. " Mountain House is simply packed out. Delegates have been pouring in all day long; our three other hotels in Caux are all full, and we've had to arrange overflow accommodation in hotels and villas down in Glion and Montreux."

We gained our room at last—number six. Lean politely offered me choice of beds, and I elected to sleep near the french windows.

" No hot water, I'm afraid," he said, indicating the fitted basin. " We're short of coal, and unless we can get some before the winter I don't know what we shall do. Germany gave us our last lot."

After I had washed, Lean led me up the stairs again, through a cafeteria and into an inner room where squads of volunteers were standing by to serve refreshments to late arrivals.

And then the introductions started. So many smiling men and women gripped my hand and bade me welcome that I could not keep track of all the names. A bowl of steaming soup was set before me by a granddaughter of Lloyd George, Mrs Michael Barrett; and presiding as joint " hostesses " at my table were the charming daughters of Colonel Hore-Ruthven, who vied with each other in proffering tea and biscuits. Before this meal was over, a hand was clapped upon my shoulder and I looked up to see another smiling face: that of James Coulter, a young Australian airman.

" I was watching out for you in the entrance hall when your coach came up," he said. " Can't think how I missed you. It's good to see you again. How are the family? "

We had met during my holiday in July, when he had been helpful in furnishing me with some facts about the Buchmanite's film-making enterprise. That he had lost not a moment in seeking me out now was typical of the friendly atmosphere prevailing at Caux. Whether it was a spurious atmosphere I had yet to determine.

Later, Lean having disappeared temporarily, Coulter appointed himself my " guide "; and I couldn't help smiling to reflect that a youngster who had piloted Sunderland flying-boats in the war should condescend to pilot *me* to my room.

He bade me good night and said he would look out for me in the morning. He had to go down to Glion to sleep, but he would be up at Mountain House quite early. He was working in the Press office.

*   *   *

I was glad to turn in after my long and crowded day. But lying upon my bedside table I found a twelve-page leaflet inscribed: WELCOME TO CAUX. They think of everything, I mused, as I started to read. " In this booklet we wish to welcome you to Caux and give you information which will be useful during your stay."

The leaflet certainly seemed a mine of information, giving the times for meals, the hours at which meetings and assemblies were held, particulars of incoming and outgoing mail, with postal rates; rates for telephone calls and telegrams; notes about hairdressing, dry-cleaning, and shoe-repairing facilities; and miniature floor plans to save visitors from losing their way.

A resident doctor and trained nurses were available, it said, a surgery being open daily.

> The Housekeepers on your floor are anxious to help you in every way [I read]. Please consult them on any needs you may have. They will be glad to provide you with anything you may need in your room.

There was a lot more, but I was weary, and decided to defer further reading until the morning. I settled down comfortably in bed and wondered when Lean would appear. The sight of a Bible upon his bedside table set me thinking. Was this room-sharing part of a deep-laid plot? Had I been put in with a high-powered member of the Council of Management for a purpose? Would he start preaching at me? Try to " change " me and so silence criticism? From snatches of doctrine I had gathered from some of the literature he had sent me I knew that the good Grouper goes after his man. I became more suspicious than ever.

Dr Buchman had an expressive phrase for the process. " It's no use throwing eye medicine out of a second-storey window," or something like that, meaning, of course, that personal evangelism implied getting the drops into each individual eye.

And just then the door opened and Lean came in, smiling as usual and not looking in the least like an evangelist. He threw off his clothes in no time; got into bed—and out again as an afterthought to wash—a rapid, unobtrusive performance—then back into bed again.

We chatted casually for a few moments, but he seemed as weary as I was. We exchanged sleepy " Good nights " and settled down. So I was not to be " changed " just yet, it seemed! But I was determined to be on my guard.

You will have noted that in spite of my pious resolves about strict impartiality I was, in these early stages of my investigation, very much on the defensive. Was I being over-cautious, over-critical? Too ready to ascribe to my Buchmanite hosts motives which were chiefly conjured up in my own imagination?

Reflection in more leisured moments told me that they, in turn, probably felt equally doubtful about me. After all, I was a stranger within their gates, a singularly inquisitive stranger, who had already asked scores of searching questions about their organization. Moreover, I was a journalist, and the Press, on the whole, had never been very kind to the Oxford Group.

Few papers or magazines seemed to think the movement worth serious consideration. When they did print anything it was seldom complimentary. The general trend seemed to be one of apathy. Some people wrote of the Group as if it were a crank cult, almost beyond the pale; others would discount its claims and damn its efforts with faint praise. How were my hosts to know that I wouldn't do the same?

So it is not surprising if my feeling of mistrust clouded some of our early exchanges; but this phase of cautious preliminary sparring eased as my probe proceeded. The Buchmanites saw, I think, that I was sincere in my quest for enlightenment, just as I came to realize that they were sparing no effort in striving to furnish me with every facility I demanded.

In my bag I had my list of twenty-eight questions and the replies to most of them which had been given to me before leaving London. Five or six queries remained unanswered, but these, you may remember, Lean had promised should be cleared up at Caux.

Also in my bag was a second typewritten list. It covered about a dozen other points which I meant to press relentlessly. On the morrow my investigation would begin in earnest.

CHAPTER 2

World's Strangest Congress

WHEN I opened my eyes in the morning I saw that my room-mate was hunched up in bed reading his Bible. Pencil and paper lay at hand, and at intervals he made certain jottings. It was his " Quiet Time." He was getting his " guidance " for the day, listening to God. I felt a trifle guilty about those suspicions I had entertained overnight.

So I lay still until Lean showed signs of stirring, then I bade him good morning. He asked if I had slept well, and I said : " Yes, thank you," which was not strictly true, for I had been overtired and had tossed about a good deal before finally settling.

" I have to go to an early meeting," he informed me as he started to dress. " So shall we meet after breakfast? You can wander up any time you like; it's a cafeteria service. There's no need to climb the stairs—you can go out through the french windows, and if you follow the path round it will bring you to the dining-hall. I'll look for you on the terrace later on."

I got up immediately he had gone. As I dressed I looked through the open french windows on to an expanse of sloping lawn. It was a little uncanny, for after all the stairs we had descended the night before I had imagined myself underground. The phenomenon was explained as soon as I stepped out into the sunlight and saw that Mountain House was built into the shoulder of the spur on which it stood.

The path Lean had mentioned lay a little to the left and, following it, I came to a gradual flight of winding steps which brought me to the cafeteria. It was an animated scene that greeted me, for swarms of people were coming and going with their breakfast trays, some seeking tables in the open, under the trees, others heading for different parts of the vast dining-hall. There were people of all ages and all nationalities: Indians in saris, turbanned Sikhs, men and women in Burmese costume, Indonesians, Nigerians, Norwegians, Germans, Austrians, Japanese, and scores of others in national dresses I could not identify. But variations in costume or colour did not seem to matter, for they all had one thing in common: they all looked serenely happy.

I joined the queue at the counter and soon helped myself to coffee and rolls and cherry jam. The choice of dishes offered was extensive: there was porridge, and cereals, and cheese, and a wide assortment of fruits. The abundance was startling for anyone coming from a rationed country; and volunteer workers were behind the counter ready to replenish any tray or dish as it became empty. Everything was of the highest quality.

Steering my way, tray in hand, in search of a vacant seat, I heard myself being hailed. I looked round and saw that it was another of my holiday acquaintances, Dr Morris Martin, one of Frank Buchman's right-hand men.

" So you're here again," he said. " Come and join us."

He introduced me to his table companions, an Austrian professor and his wife. The professor hastened to relieve me of my tray and carry it back to the rack; his wife, observing that I had spilled some coffee into my saucer, rushed to get me another cup. They had caught the spirit of Caux.

I had put on an old school tie, which Dr Martin was quick to notice, for we had discovered at our previous meeting that we were both Old Merchant Taylors'. Indeed, we had joked about it, for my son, another OMT, had been with me then, and on our fleeting visit to the film studio in Lausanne, we had run into a fourth. " Nearly as ubiquitous as Buchmanites," I had said.

There was little opportunity for conversation as Martin had to whisk his charges off to an early meeting; but he was interested in my mission. Not long before, he himself had gone to America to beg free paper to enable some German supporters of Moral Re-Armament to publish a handbook. Just like that, it seemed! Paper was wanted for " the cause," so a key man was sent across the Atlantic to get it. That was something that could not be laughed off. It confirmed the world-wide scope and influence of Dr Buchman's movement.[1]

Evidence of superb organization was around me now in the way in which the crowds of happy people came and went. There was no confusion or fuss; no one seemed lost; everything went smoothly. I couldn't help contrasting it with the scene that meets the traveller at Calais, where loud-speakers blare continuously and where police, Customs officers, railway officials, and couriers from a dozen travel companies seem unable to reduce much smaller crowds to order.

Here at Mountain House, notwithstanding the mixture of races and tongues, there was no chaos such as may be seen at any busy port. The precision was uncanny. There were no men with megaphones; no loud-speakers; no conspicuous notices. A mixed crowd, numbering thousands, seemed to find language bars no handicap and to fall into the " help yourself " routine harmoniously.

*   *   *

Sauntering into the open again, I made for the terrace. But half-way across the lawn I turned to take in the

[1] Swedish supporters and paper manufacturers also contributed generously, and shipping and haulage firms of other nations provided free transportation, I was told.

grandeur of Mountain House. Its towers and minarets had a fairy-story, dream-palace air which made the polyglot crowds far from incongruous. In the days when, as the Caux Palace Hotel, it was a haunt of the wealthy, Edgar Wallace spent holidays there with his family.

Margaret Lane, his biographer, has told how little those holidays varied from his ordinary working life in London.

> The dictaphone was always set up in his hotel sitting-room as soon as he arrived, and one or other of his secretaries was always included in the large party of family and friends which he took with him. While the others enjoyed their winter sports by day and dancing by night Edgar, a little sorry for himself and consequently in difficult temper, would work in his steam-heated room with the windows closed. . . .

I thought of this and tried to picture that old master of thrillers in this setting, pouring fantasy into the mouth-piece of his dictaphone. His most improbable yarns, I felt, must have been more credible than the story of Mountain House today.

Crossing to the terrace, I stood for a long time gazing down upon the splendid vista spread out below: the slopes of Glion and Les Avants, the roofs of Montreux and Territet, the vast lake and the pin-point steamers, and, far away to the left, Villeneuve, and, beyond, the mouth of the Rhône.

It was easy, scanning the near shore, to pick out the familiar outline of the Castle of Chillon. In its historic great hall, I had heard, the Government of Vaud, the canton in which Caux lies, had staged a banquet in Dr Buchman's honour. At the doorway through which tourists flock in their thousands every summer, the founder of the Oxford Group had been met by the Vice-President of the Vaud State Council and the mayors of Montreux and Veytaux. And he had been given a seat of honour, with the Swiss flag draped behind him. The banqueting hall, hung with rare tapestries and lit by candles for the occasion, provided a setting of unmatched impressiveness. I had seen a picture of this gathering, and among my papers I had a clipping which quoted the Mayor as saying:

> We Swiss are proud to have this world centre for Moral Re-Armament on our soil. To triumph over wars, social struggles, and all the difficulties that surround us—these are your aims, and in achieving them we are united behind you.

Well, that, too, could not be laughed off. And there were reams and reams of circumstantial evidence of a similar nature included in that dossier Lean had prepared so diligently for my benefit. But still I was far from convinced that the Moral Re-Armament scheme, attractive as it was in many ways, could be accepted at its face value.

I studied some of the delegates dotted about on seats along the terrace. Many, I noticed, were having their "Quiet Time," note-books open on their knee, pencils in hand. They might have been ordinary people making up their diaries.

A sudden desire for a cigarette seized me, but no one else in all that throng was smoking. I strolled to the far end of the terrace before lighting up, and then I felt like a guilty schoolboy retiring behind the cricket pavilion or the gym for a furtive puff! "This is quite ridiculous," I said to myself, but I still felt slightly embarrassed.

Then, pulling myself together, I brought out some of my papers and began to study them. To refresh my mind I ran through some of the questions and the answers Lean had given me. I had asked whether Mountain House ranked as a "branch" and how it stood in relation to the British and American headquarters. It seemed there was a separate registration for Switzerland— Fondation du Réarmement Morale. "It is legally quite independent," ran Lean's reply, "and covers the operation of Mountain House and the other hotels at Caux."

Dr Buchman receives the Grand Cross of the Order of Merit, the highest German decoration, at New Delhi, India.

[Associated Press

Dr Buchman, with some of the delegates from thirty-eight countries, at the World Assembly for Moral Re-Armament, at Caux, Switzerland.

At my request he had given me full details of its purchase. Requisitioned by the Swiss authorities during the
war, it had been used to shelter internees and refugees
and, as is the case with requisitioned property the world
over, it had deteriorated sadly. So much so, in fact, that
after the war there had been talk of pulling it down and
selling the furniture and fittings abroad. Then the Swiss
Buchmanites had stepped in and acquired it for the
bargain price of £80,000. Lean pointed out that the
retaining wall under the terrace could not even be built
for that figure today. Indeed, the price was less than a
bid that a French company had made in the hope of
securing the fittings and furniture for resale in France.

How, then, did this miracle happen? Why did the
Swiss authorities accept the lower offer? According to
Lean, their reason was twofold. They were prompted
first by the desirability of keeping the hotel as a going
concern. A costly mountain railway, built in the prosperous days of tourism, had to be kept going for the sake of
a few inhabitants scattered about the mountain-side. If
Caux ceased to be a flourishing centre, the railway could
not prosper; far better, then, sell the hotel at a knock-out
price in the hope that visitors would come in sufficient
numbers to keep Caux on the map.

The gamble has come off. These World Assemblies
must gladden the Government's heart. Because of the
thousands who now flock yearly to Mountain House
the railway is even able to grant reduced fares to the
visitors !

But the secondary consideration, Lean assured me, was
the Government's conviction that the work of Moral
Re-Armament could be one of Switzerland's major
contributions to the world today. " Successive Presidents
of the Confederation," he assured me, " have said this on
their official visits to Caux."

C

All right, then, you say. The Buchmanites got a bargain. But £80,000 is still a lot of money. Where did that money come from? Here is the answer I was given: " The money comes from all over Switzerland. It comes from Swiss people, many of whom have felt that this was their best opportunity of showing their gratitude for having been spared the horrors of war."

But, having made the purchase, the Buchmanites were faced with the almost overwhelming task of putting the premises, long-neglected, into serviceable condition. They were anxious to have it ready for an assembly in 1946, though experts assured them that such a feat would be impossible.

Still, volunteer helpers were mobilized by the hundred; craftsmen, engineers, students, and others set to work, clearing debris, repairing woodwork, overhauling electrical appliances, putting the plumbing in order, staining, painting, distempering, polishing. While men tackled these varied tasks, self-organized squads of women scrubbed and sewed so that curtains, bedding, and table linen could be ready for the opening.

Only a people fired by a quite abnormal zeal, I reflected, could have worked like that. And they had confounded the experts. The palatial new headquarters became a reality; the grandiose dream materialized. Each year these fanatical workers, their ranks swollen by other willing helpers, added improvements. Each year had seen bigger and better Assemblies, and this year's looked like eclipsing anything that had gone before.

Substantial credits, I felt, had to be marked up to my hosts on this account.

Yet, even with this wealth of volunteer labour, it was patent that considerable sums must be needed to maintain a headquarters of such magnificence. I had asked about this and had been told that Mountain House cost 15,000 francs a day to run. Offerings poured in just as they had done for the purchase. Besides cash donations there had been a world-wide response with gifts in kind. At my request, Lean had furnished me with a list of these. It was staggering.

Australia had sent 2 gross of glass tumblers. Canada had provided 5 tons of flour. Supporters in Denmark had sent 100,000 eggs and 150 kgs of butter. From Egypt had come cotton to be woven into sheets. France had sent 900 knives and 600 dusters. Finland, 1,000 glass plates, 200 kgs of cheese, and 400 folding chairs. Germany had provided 200 tons of coke, while British supporters had given 71 blankets, 80 coffee and hot-water pots, a carpet, matting, and chinaware. The carpet in the dining-room, I learned, had come from Holland, while Italy had sent honey and rice, and Jamaica 3 tons of sugar. There had been a ton of coffee from Kenya, as well as 240 kgs of tea. Sweden had sent teaspoons and glassware; America, 3 tons of miscellaneous foodstuffs and quantities of gabardine cloth. Swiss friends had given potatoes, curtain material, and 2,000 sheets.

Why, I pondered to myself, had this remarkable international effort not been noticed in the newspapers?

Sitting there upon the terrace, reviewing these points, I brought out my "Welcome to Caux" leaflet for closer perusal. Amenities, I found, included a Travel Bureau and a Currency Office where travellers' cheques could be cashed. Mountain House was, in fact, a self-contained unit, catering for all possible needs and seemingly anticipating the wishes of its guests.

One of my queries, left unanswered in London, had concerned the organization at Caux. To stage-manage an Assembly of such magnitude must entail colossal effort, I had argued, and I had asked who did it all.

"That you will discover at Caux," Lean had assured

me, and now, in the leaflet, I found a section headed:
" How the Work is Done."   Here it is:

> A distinctive feature of Caux is the way in which Moral
> Re-Armament is seen in action throughout the running of the
> houses.
> The work behind the Assembly gives an opportunity to
> test the truths given from platform and stage in practical ways,
> and to draw on the experience of men and women from many
> lands who have learned to apply them. A hundred teachers,
> as well as business men, labour leaders, army officers, house-
> wives, students, and many others are among those who have
> come at their own expense and with a sense of privilege, to give
> long hours of work in servicing the Assembly. They are
> interesting people to meet. They will greatly welcome your
> help from time to time, since keeping house for a thousand
> people needs many hands at certain times of the day. You will
> enjoy the experience of working with them.
> Your help will be welcomed by the Cooks and the Vegetable
> team, by the Dining Room service teams, the Cleaning and
> Wash-up teams and the Housekeepers. If you would like to
> help, for whatever period you wish, please inform the Reception
> Office and you will be put in touch with the right person.

So that was the secret of the smooth running of Mountain House. Everyone lent a hand, and many hands
made light work. The volunteers who had stood by to
minister to myself and fellow travellers the night before
had been part of the system.

Another section of this informative leaflet was headed
" How Much Does It Cost." It, too, deserves to be set
down verbatim.

> Caux has been created and is maintained through the sacrifice
> of those who believe in the answer which Moral Re-Armament
> can bring to the nations, and which is beyond price. Many
> have given all they possess to make Caux available.
> Naturally, in the present state of Europe, many come to
> Caux who cannot contribute financially, but for whom it is
> right and necessary to be here. No fixed charge, therefore, is
> made for those attending the Assembly, but if every person were
> able to make his contribution it would average about S. Fr. 150
> a week.
> Those who can bring currency are asked to base their con-
> tributions on this figure. Payments, and gifts on behalf of guests

who cannot bring money, as well as gifts towards the general expenses of the Assembly and Moral Re-Armament, can be made at any time at the Reception Office or at the Currency Office.

Well, this was frank enough, and I approved the business-like way in which it was set forth; but something dawned upon me and caused me to run through the entire leaflet again. Curious, I thought, but there is no mention anywhere of the Oxford Group. I looked again to make sure. No. It was all " Moral Re-Armament." Why this inconsistency? And why had Swiss Buch-manites registered themselves as Fondation du Réarme-ment Morale, when their companions in Britain were registered as The Oxford Group? I made a note to look into that when an opportunity arose.

I was just pocketing my papers again when Garth Lean and James Coulter came striding towards me. They asked how I had been faring, and I told them how I had breakfasted with Dr Martin.

" I'm so glad you found someone like that," said Lean. " He's an excellent fellow."

We stood, leaning upon the rail, chatting and enjoying the view. I complimented my friends upon their superb headquarters and asked when it had been built.

" I'm not quite sure," said Lean, " but Mussolini is supposed to have had a hand in building this wall when he was working in Switzerland as a labourer."

* * *

A little later that morning I attended a Press conference and renewed acquaintanceship with Reginald Holme, one of the Press officers who had shepherded me during my holiday visit. I thought he seemed surprised that I should have deemed it necessary to return on a probing mission; but he shook my hand warmly enough and inquired after my family in the kindest terms. A Winchester scholar,

Holme has been with Dr Buchman for many years, principally in America. His wife, also an ardent Buchmanite, is in charge of a cake-baking team at Mountain House. He told me they had made their home in Switzerland and had a chalet a little way down the mountain-side.

The conference was sparsely attended, but the East was noticeably represented, there being Pressmen from Pakistan and Burma, the latter including U Tun Nyoe, Chief Editor of *The Burma Tribune*.

Garth Lean, presiding, explained that as the Assembly we should be attending shortly would include industrial speakers, and as coal was the key to all industry, he proposed to tell us something of what had been achieved by Moral Re-Armament teams in the British coalfields.

Remarkable results, he declared, had been secured both in the Rhondda and in North Staffordshire. A committee, headed by the Lord Mayor of Cardiff and the Lord Lieutenant of Glamorgan, and whose members included workers and employers, had invited a team to South Wales with their play, *The Forgotten Factor*. A two-months tour had resulted, and it had been accompanied by enthusiastic demonstrations everywhere.

I have never seen this play presented, but, from all the accounts I have read, I gather that it is a dramatic portrayal of conflict between masters and men.

Being a propaganda play, especially written by Alan Thornhill, formerly Fellow and Chaplain of Hertford College, Oxford, it demonstrates how Moral Re-Armament theories, if put into practice, can bring about harmony in industry.

Here is a typical sample of dialogue, taken from a scene in which a subversive agent invades an owner's house with strikers he is leading. Finding himself confronted by his union leader, he is reasoned with like this: " Don't think I wouldn't like to have it out with you, Joe Bush! But these days we've got to act different. It's not who's right that matters, but what's right!"

And in another scene there is a passage between the employer and the union leader, the employer saying: "I'm sorry, Rankin, I've made you my enemy when you might have been my friend. You brought something new with you when you came in here. It's trust . . . and honesty . . . but it's more than that. It's the forgotten factor!"

It sounds like something from *Good Words* or *Sunday At Home*, vintage 1890, but lest you think I have unfairly torn these quotations from their context, let me assure you that they are lifted straight from the Group's own publicity matter. In any case, the laugh is on anyone who may feel inclined to scoff because, as Lean explained to the Press conference, production figures had soared in every area where the play had been shown.

Before me at the moment is a statement signed by the Lord Mayor of Cardiff and the Chairman of the Rhondda UDC. It contains the following declaration:

> When we saw *The Forgotten Factor* at the Westminster Theatre, we determined that it must come to South Wales. We were certain that its message of sound homes, revolutionary teamwork in industry, and unity in the nation would stir a great response in our people. Other prominent citizens felt the same, and united with us to invite the play to our area. We can say that wherever the play has been, homes have been made happier, co-operation has developed in industry and our democratic life has been strengthened.

From the same source I have culled the fact that the players, like an advancing army, " lived on the country." Four hundred families gave free board to the cast. Theatre owners, printers, caterers, and others gave special terms and facilities as " a form of national service." Other expenses were met by gifts from many thousands of people who saw the play.

And here is a statement from Bill Yates, the miner from North Staffordshire, who was present, you may remember, on the occasion of my second interview with Groupers in London.

> The wife and I used not to agree. We were on the edge of breaking up. And I took my unhappiness to the pit. So when we met, the manager and I used to do a good deal of banging the table. There was constant trouble.
> Then I went to see *The Forgotten Factor*. We got things straight at home. I went to the manager and said: "Let's run this pit the MRA way." He agreed—and the men like it much better. We have not had a single row or stoppage since then. The increased output is due to the new honesty and unselfishness introduced by MRA.

Of course, Garth Lean did not tell the Press conference all this. I am giving you the benefit of information gathered piecemeal in the prolonged inquiries which had preceded my flight to Switzerland. In this way you will be better able to appreciate the many-sided nature of the investigation to which I was committed.

My notes at this stage were piling up under various headings, such as: "Present Activities," "Mountain House," "Assemblies," "Organization and Finances," "Propaganda," "Personalities," "History and Evolution," "Work in Industry," "World Scope," and "Future Plans."

It was only by tabulating items of information as I went along that I could cope with the fresh avenues of inquiry which kept opening up before me. Garth Lean's secretary had generously offered her services, which I appreciated as a thoughtful gesture; but I preferred to work alone, making brief code notes in my own unorthodox shorthand whenever I got the chance. I was grateful, though, for her assistance in gathering various reports and statistics relating to past Assemblies, and Lean, Coulter, and Holme gave me similar help.

*   *   *

A dark, good-looking man, wearing a well-cut navy suit, nodded to me across the Press table. That was the only contact I had with Peter Howard, one of the Oxford Group's star writers. There was an understanding light in his eyes, and perhaps the flicker of a smile playing upon his lips. I guessed what was in his mind at that moment.

You will remember that several of Peter Howard's books had been included in the special dossier which Lean had prepared for my edification. They had proved both valuable and interesting, for, as one of Buchmanism's leading advocates, he wrote with tremendous fervour and a great deal of intimacy.

Being semi-confessional in character, his books provided a first-hand testimony of his experience of Buchmanism. That this was considerable may be assumed from the fact that it has provided him with material for five or six books, all of them best-sellers.

I was particularly interested in the testimony he had to give regarding his experiments in " listening to God." As this was the peg upon which the whole structure of Buchmanism seemed to hang I followed all that Peter Howard had to say on the subject with more than ordinary care. Indeed, I re-read some passages through several times to make sure that I was not misinterpreting the author's words.

The net results, I'm afraid, were sadly disappointing. But, on reflection, I am prepared to concede that some measure of fault may have lain with me for expecting too much. I had thought to light upon some stimulating revelation, but the instances cited by Howard were so ordinary as to be almost banal in their simplicity.

First thing in the morning he would sit with paper and pencil before him " to listen to God," ready to jot down the thoughts which came to him. One example of

" guidance " which he records at length started with the thought : " Pay Sergeant Smith the £5 you owe him."

Smith was a masseur in Oxford who charged £5 a term for his services to University athletes. Howard had left Oxford without paying and had forgotten the debt for about ten years until " guidance " brought it back to his memory. " Some people," he writes, " may explain it away as a subconscious thought of a debt which had been nagging at me all those years. I don't think so. I did not worry very much about £5 debts."

Anyway, Peter Howard, " a little startled by this message," contacted the Sergeant and settled the debt.

Some time later he received " guidance " in which the message "Write to Jacks " was reiterated. Jacks, he explains, was the headmaster of his old school. He interpreted this " guidance " as indicating that he ought to refund a Board of Education grant made at a time when he had thought of becoming a schoolmaster.

He tells how he argued with himself that there was no obligation for him to refund this money; but, all the same, he wrote as " guided," asked how much had been advanced and whether he could be held legally responsible. He added that he now thought he was under a moral obligation to pay back this money. A reply came saying the sum involved was £218, but that he was correct in assuming that no legal onus lay upon him to make a refund. In spite of this he decided to send a cheque.

> It is strange how, before I met the Group [he records], I would have worried and brooded and felt resentful for weeks if I had had to pay out so large a sum, even in payment for some self-indulgent luxury like a motor-car or a television set. . . . I was beginning to know that guidance was right. . . .

But Howard did not confine these experiments in " listening to God " to himself. He records quite solemnly how he and his wife decided that their children must be given the chance of listening, too. The eldest, then aged seven, was able to write down the " guidance " for himself (they all had books), the others had theirs recorded for them.

This system, Howard declares, " made a great difference to our children." Then he tells how one morning his four-year-old daughter refused to drink her milk. " She yelled and yelled and yelled," until her seven-year-old brother, playing in the next room, left his toys and coaxed her into drinking her milk. Questioned about this, the boy said he had " had the thought " that it was his job and nobody else's to stop his little sister from crying.

Howard's comment on this is: " I recommend the Oxford Group way of life to those who really want their children to get a sense of responsibility for their own place in the household."

I have taken these illustrations from Howard's book: *Innocent Men*, of which, I am told, 155,000 copies have been sold. Do you wonder that I was disappointed? Yet the author seems to have been disappointed, too, for to do him full justice, he states in the same volume: " Some people in the Group have received the most remarkable and dramatic pieces of guidance from God. . . . I have no such dramatic experiences to offer for your consideration."

Nevertheless, the fact that his own experiments proved so unrewarding in no wise diminished his faith.

There was a time when he was one of Lord Beaverbrook's bright young men, writing to order for his chief, sometimes being hauled from his bed at 2 a.m. to do so. But it was not as a fellow-journalist that he greeted me across the table in the Press Room at Caux that morning. There was more behind his nod than that.

Why did I read significance into that nod and the flickering suspicion of a smile? Because I knew from his books that his first approach to the Oxford Group had been made with the calculated aim of securing an exclusive " inside " story. Like the fools of Goldsmith's *Deserted Village* he had gone to scoff and had " remain'd to pray." The Buchmanites had " changed " him overnight!

Would the same thing happen to me?

CHAPTER 3

" *People are More Important than Things* "

THE dictum is Dr Buchman's, and long before that first full day of my stay at Mountain House was over, I began to grasp exactly what it implied. For all their varied costumes and tongues, the happy delegates might have been one people. Some miracle had effected a harmony that is difficult to describe.

I got this impression immediately we left the Press Room and made our way to the huge Assembly Hall, where delegates were gathering for the morning session. Everyone seemed to be lending a hand, some carrying chairs from the adjoining theatre, others arranging them in rows. If they had been drilled and rehearsed in these tasks they could not have performed them with more dispatch.

As we settled into our seats, waiting for the meeting to begin, the vast room seemed vibrant with goodwill. Some subtle force had been generated—a quality, alas! too often lacking from international gatherings of diplomats, statesmen, and more orthodox would-be peace-makers—a readiness to forget nationalistic pride and racial prejudice. Yes! It looked as if Dr Buchman's slogan was right. People *are* more important than things.

And how widely he had cast his net to gather so many contrasting types under one roof. Consulting lists of delegates which had been supplied at my request, I read that they included twenty-seven Cabinet Ministers in office and 118 Members of Parliament from twenty-six nations.

Student leaders were there from America, Britain, Burma, Czechoslovakia, France, Germany, Holland,

South Africa, and Scandinavia. And trades union chiefs from thirty-five countries were rubbing shoulders with chiefs of employers' associations who were represented just as strongly.

My invitation leaflet furnished evidence of the world-wide interest focused upon the Assembly. Robert Schuman, Foreign Minister of France, had sent a message to Dr Buchman which was said to set the keynote of the proceedings.

> In the economic field we have the Marshall Plan. In the field of security we have the Atlantic Pact. Now we need to give ideological content to the lives of the millions of Europe. We must reach the people so that the Pact will be sustained by a deep change in the way of life of the Western world, through a real spiritual renewal.

Other messages were quoted as coming from Dr Karl Arnold, Minister-president of North Rhine-Westphalia, Germany, Igino Giordani, Member of the Italian Parliament and Editor of *Fides*, General Henri Guisan, war-time Commander-in-Chief of the Swiss Army, Senator Karl E. Mundt, as co-chairman of the Smith-Mundt Committee, United States Congress, Sir Zafrullah Khan, Foreign Minister of Pakistan, Sir Patrick Dollan, former Lord Provost of Glasgow and Editor of the Scottish *Daily Herald*, and Dr Hans Boekler, Chairman of the Trade Union Congress of the British Zone, Germany.

All these messages spoke glowingly of a belief that the power of Moral Re-Armament would cement international understanding. You can imagine, then, with what expectation I looked forward to that morning's session. It gave me my first glimpse of Dr Buchman since my arrival. He sat out in front at one side of the hall, his back to the tall windows, one eye on the platform, the other upon the audience, watching, Janus-like, all comings and goings.

As people settled in their seats a pianist played cheerful

music. Chairman and speakers were ranged upon a low platform, with a massed choir, formed by the Mackinac Singers and various national choruses, grouped behind them.

I must tell you something about the Mackinac Singers. They have formed what Dr Buchman would call " a spearhead " in Moral Re-Armament campaigns in all parts of the world. Trained to a high pitch of efficiency, they are used with tremendous effect to create just the right emotional atmosphere. Most people appreciate fine singing, and the Mackinac Singers give of their best. Though they have performed a thousand times, their zeal is in no wise diminished. Their diction is faultless and every song is " put over " with a gusto which seems spontaneous. Their eyes sparkle and their faces are illumined. Their vitality seems unflagging.

Music ranks with the Buchmanites as a weapon. " It can excite or calm, inflame, or heal," they claim. " It can be a great, inspiring lifting force." And they use it on every possible occasion, and with studied ingenuity.

I was soon to find that a song had been specially written to meet every conceivable eventuality. If a Welsh miner was to speak, perhaps to testify how coal output had soared under the influence of Moral Re-Armament in the Valleys, he would be greeted with the rousing *Rhondda Song*. Similarly, the announcement that a Scottish shipyard worker was about to speak, would be the choir's cue for the equally inspiring *Clydeside Song*. And a Member of Parliament, just arrived from London, would be hailed with the *Westminster Song*.

I knew something about this propaganda use of music by the Buchmanites, for on my holiday I had heard a German chorus render a plaintive Japanese song to welcome delegates from the Far East. The gracious tribute delighted everyone, and Reginald Holme, who was beside me at the time, said that Japanese had told him that when they closed their eyes and listened they could not believe it was not their own countrymen who were singing.

This morning's meeting opened with the Chairman inviting newly arrived delegates to stand up as called upon. We did so, country by country, each party being warmly applauded by the others. Especially sustained applause greeted one lone delegate who made a conspicuous figure as he stood up in his picturesque Burmese dress. Instantly Dr Buchman leapt to his feet and beckoned. " Come over here! " he shouted across the hall. As the visitor threaded his way round to take a seat at Buchman's side, the applause became deafening and people rose to their feet in their enthusiasm.

That lone delegate was U Ba Lwin, a distinguished educationalist attending the Assembly as the personal representative of Burma's Prime Minister, U Thakin Nu.

As a sample of the speeches delivered that morning I cannot do better than quote from the testimony of two ex-Communists: Mr Max Bladeck, Works Council, Rheinpreussen Mines, the Ruhr, and Mr Jack Jones, South Wales miner and steelworker. All speeches were delivered sentence by sentence, an interpreter standing beside the speaker and following up with a free translation. English speakers always had their words translated into German in this way, and French and German speakers were similarly followed up in English.

One of the German interpreters was Franz Junghans, a Messerschmidt fighter-pilot in the war and now, at twenty-nine, proud to stand beside former enemies to render this service in the cause of Moral Re-Armament. He says he finds the fight to bring an ideology of freedom to the world is more exciting than diving into a group of bombers. His compatriot, Max Bladeck, claimed that he had been a good fighter, too—for Communism. Now he fights for MRA.

" The meaning and purpose of this ideology," he said that morning, " is to produce for mankind a world where people are not at enmity and where all contradictions are ruled out. In what way will it help the world, if we have a war between East and West and the East or West triumphs and plants its flag on top of the ruins, and the people are no longer there?

" That is why I have changed myself. I simply turned to reason and reality. I have already changed a number of other Communists."

He added that it was up to leading industrialists and statesmen to change themselves and, by changing themselves, to change their countries and their surroundings. " I say to all present, take the ideology of Frank Buchman seriously, because it is the only ideology which can bring peace and happiness to mankind."

The most fiery speech of the morning, I thought, came from the other ex-Communist, Jack Jones.

" I come from the part of Britain which is called ' Little Moscow '," he declared amid laughter. " I worked in the mines of that area and was forced through an injury, after twenty-eight years, to leave the mines. I had been training the miners in the ideology of Communism.

" I went to work in the steel industry, and within nine months I became the trade union representative in the department in which I worked. I knew nothing about steel. But I knew enough about revolution to defeat any industrialist. I knew also how to use men in a revolution. . . . I was determined to break a record which the steel industry held—fifty years of peace. . . . As a Communist I did not believe in letting people rest, and I was determined to disturb everybody and anybody.

" Any Communist worth his salt will defeat an army
D

of industrialists without an ideology. And when I went into the office of the manager for the first time I thought I was entering a place where this fellow did not have an ideology.

" On my entry into the office, for the first time in my industrial life I was asked to sit down. They generally handed me my hat and asked me to go. And when the manager asked me if I had ever approached a problem in the light of *what's* right instead of *who's* right, I began to get nervous, because I believed that every manager who spoke about fair play was either mad or a crook. I decided that this fellow was mentally sick, so I suggested that we left our problem till the morrow; he might feel better then."

He went on to tell us how he'd spent a disturbed night, unable to sleep for pondering over the problem of " What is right." He went back to work next day determined to upset the manager " because a trained Communist knows that if he can get his opponent to lose his head he has won the victory. But," he went on, " I found that this manager had found the very thing for which I had been searching all my life. He had found that the only answer to every industrial problem, every economic problem, every political problem, every domestic problem, rested in personal change.

" I tried to change a system. I now realize through meeting a superior ideology that a system is a set of events which are determined by individuals. If we want to change a system we must change ourselves."

The only thing to stop the onrush of materialism, he said in conclusion, was Moral Re-Armament, personal change and sacrifice. " As a former Communist I stand with Max Bladeck, united with anybody of any nation who will fight with us to keep the world free."

I left the Assembly Hall interested, but not greatly

impressed, for I had heard little that I had not read a dozen times in the literature I had accumulated in my quest. But more interesting developments lay ahead. I had expressed a desire to meet someone who had been with the Oxford Group from the time of its inception, so that I could gather facts concerning its early history at first hand.

Garth Lean had promised he would see what he could do about this, and after a brief disappearance he rejoined me with the news that I was to lunch with Loudon Hamilton—the man in whose rooms at Oxford the whole thing had started twenty-eight years ago.

* * *

I liked Loudon Hamilton from the moment of our first cordial handshake. The fact that he was being trotted out as an exhibit at the request of an inquisitive stranger didn't seem to embarrass him in the least. I suppose he must have told his " story " a thousand times, yet he was perfectly willing to go over all the ground for my benefit and to answer all my queries.

A table had been specially reserved for us in " the little dining-room " which is set aside for such contingencies. It was another example of the thoughtful organization which lay behind the Assembly. Dr Buchman, I noticed, as we filed in, had a big table at one end where he was entertaining a number of chosen guests. As on the night of my arrival, food was served by volunteer helpers, young Groupers who appeared to be getting a great deal of fun out of it. Like everyone at Mountain House, they were noticeably cheerful. They were efficient, too, and both the food and the service were of a class to match that of a first-rate hotel.

Not that I was able to take in much of my surroundings, for I was determined not to miss a word of Hamilton's story. Garth Lean had gone to the trouble of presenting me with this opportunity, and it would be invaluable in helping me to piece together a comprehensive picture of Buchmanism.

" Now, how would you like to set about this? " asked Hamilton over the soup. " Would you like to fire a few questions at me, or what? "

I guessed that Lean had probably told him of those interviews we had had in Charles Street and had warned him to prepare for cross-questioning, but I quickly re-assured him.

" What I would really like," I told him, " would be to hear your story in your own words. I understand that you were in at the very beginning of the Oxford Group; that you were then a student at Christchurch, and that it was actually in your rooms in Peckwater Quad that the first gathering was held? "

" That's quite correct," assented Hamilton.

" Well, if you wouldn't mind going on from there, it would be perfect. I'm genuinely interested in learning all I can about the Group and its beginnings."

" All right, then," said Hamilton, and he plunged into his story without any further preamble.

He began by painting a vivid picture of life at the University after World War I, when about ninety per cent of the undergraduates were ex-officers, from majors down-ward, just back from the midst of exciting adventures and trying to resume their studies in an unsettled post-war world. These veterans of twenty-one or twenty-two were wise in some things, yet disillusioned and perplexed. Some had brilliant Service records behind them; some had rows of decorations, but all that counted for nothing now. It had been called the " war to end wars "; but no one believed it; the world was still in a mess.

" Some of us formed ourselves into a ' Beer and

Beefsteak Society,' " said Hamilton. " We used to meet and hold lengthy debates and argue and advance our pet theories on all that was wrong with the world and how we would put it right. You can picture us puffing away at our pipes, swapping ideas till the small hours of the morning, and doubtless consuming vast quantities of liquor! I don't know that we ever reached any decisions about anything, but we certainly talked a lot. Some wit once remarked that in Oxford we don't always stop talking when we have finished what we have to say.

" Anyway, one summer evening—this was in 1921, by the way—a friend of mine, a Rhodes scholar, ran into me in the quad and asked me if I'd care to meet a man from Cambridge. I said: ' Yes,' and that was my first introduction to Frank. He was a man of middle size with manners and clothes that gave no clue to his job, but his eyes were large and alert.

" I don't think I was particularly impressed at that first meeting. More from politeness than anything we invited him to attend one of our fortnightly philosophic gatherings. He came, but no one took very much notice of him, and he just sat silent and aloof, listening to us all talking. At first it was a serious evening, in the wrong sense. The occasion was a philosophic debate, we became very profound. But Frank just sat silent."

Eleven o'clock came, and still the visitor had said nothing, Hamilton went on. But somewhere towards the tail end of the proceedings one of the debaters, rather as an act of condescension, invited the stranger to speak. The moment the American began talking the atmosphere seemed to change. He picked up some thread of the discussion and used it to weave his pattern, holding his listeners' attention, it seems, by the original ideas he began to expound. In untheological language he began to tell about " changed " lives.

" He described the changes in men so like ourselves that interest was riveted at once. And the odd thing about him was his ability to talk quite freely and naturally to us—the beer and beefsteakers, remember!—of things which the average Englishman *never* mentions. At least, he finds it hard to talk of such things without self-consciousness or some show of embarrassment.

" Frank could discuss spiritual matters and use God's name as naturally as if he were talking of everyday affairs."

Loudon Hamilton told me all this over that luncheon in Mountain House as if the scene were still fresh in his mind. He almost made me feel the magnetism with which Buchman had succeeded in holding the attention of those old young men. And he must have had magnetism to make them forget their pipes and their drinks and their debate. Hamilton made it clear to me that it was not just tolerant politeness that made those undergraduates give the stranger their attention. He really held them. When they finally dispersed in the early hours of the morning, Hamilton's own enthusiasm was so fired that he at once made a breakfast appointment with the American.

A week or two later Buchman came back to Oxford, this time with three undergraduates from Cambridge. The young men were eager to tell of all their contact with Buchman had meant to them. " They weren't the type one usually associates with religious enthusiasm," said Hamilton. " Two were ex-officers and the other was a Rugger Blue."

These visitors, exhibiting a subtle yet distinctly noticeable radiance, spoke easily and naturally of a new power that had come into their lives to help them with their problems. And even though it just " wasn't done " to talk about personal religion, the hosts were deeply impressed. Hamilton said: " Their words were the words

of honest men out to share something good with anyone
who had the sense to receive it."

After that there was a lot of discussion about this
phenomenon. The interest spread, first throughout
Christchurch, and then through the whole university.
" In those early days," Hamilton told me, " it was quite
a common thing for undergraduates to queue up for hours
simply to get a few moments alone with Buchman for a
chat."

The American's influence was so great that many of
the young men he drew to him then have worked with him
for life. Hamilton told me that though he became a
master at Eton, he never lost touch with Buchman, and
eventually threw up his teaching career in order to devote
all his energies to the Group.

That luncheon passed very rapidly for me. I ate
mechanically without noticing what was placed before
me, so absorbed was I in Hamilton's narrative. Here,
I felt, was a testimony of immense value. It gave me a
picture of the Group's beginnings in a nutshell.

" Now, are you quite sure there are no questions you
want to ask? " pressed Hamilton.

Laughingly I assured him that I had facts enough, and
when I had thanked him warmly for his help, we shook
hands and parted.

* * *

Alone for a few moments, I drifted into the bookshop
at Mountain House, where I found a very wide range of
MRA publications on sale. Browsing through the shelves
I came upon a copy of *Escape to Live*, by Edward Howell.

The name struck a chord somewhere in the recesses of
memory, and as I glanced through the blurb on the
dust cover, I recalled why. The author was Wing-
Commander Edward Howell, OBE, DFC, and I was

able to place him as one of the men to whom I had been introduced when Reginald Holme was showing me round with my family earlier in the summer.

I remembered now that Holme had mentioned Howell's experience and had recommended the book as " a good adventure story, apart from anything else." The copy I held in my hand was the last one, apparently, so I hastened to secure it. But the lady behind the sale counter seemed a little dubious.

" I don't think this is for sale," she said. " It's an autographed copy." She opened the cover to show me. On top of the map of the Middle East which formed the end papers was written: " With the Author's best wishes —Edward Howell." " I don't think I can let you have this," said the assistant. " He may have signed it for somebody. I'll see if there's another." She searched for a moment or two and shook her head sadly.

" I'm afraid it's the last one," she said.

I pressed her to let me have it, telling her that I had met the author. In the end she consented, and I bore it away with a sense of triumph.

Crowds were coming and going, as they always are at Mountain House, yet the first person I ran into on leaving the bookshop was Howell himself! I reminded him of our previous meeting and showed him my purchase.

" They didn't want to let me have it at first," I explained. " It's an autographed copy, and they thought you might have signed it specially for someone else. Anyway, I've got it; and I don't want to part with it."

Howell grinned—an attractively boyish grin—and said it was quite all right. I was welcome to keep that copy.

When I examined it more closely another familiar name leapt to my eye—that of Morris Martin, my breakfast-table companion of that morning. He had contributed some verses on the fly-leaf:

In the blue Cretan sky a lone flier fighting,
    The last upholder of the free,
Falls, and an unseen finger writing,
    Marks, marks him for liberty.
Past the dim edge of serfdom and of dying,
    An imperious whisper led
Through suffering, danger-star its light supplying—
    Home, home from the dead.
Who have escaped to live, immortal band,
    Set now your nations free,
Take God's great sword of freedom in your hand
    And strike, strike for Liberty.

These lines of Dr Martin's presage the story which follows, and although I had no opportunity of reading the book until after my return to London, it is appropriate, I think, to interpolate Howell's story here.

He was sent to Crete to take over the remnant of a Hurricane squadron which had been withdrawn from Greece. He had never piloted a Hurricane before, but he could hardly admit that. Spitfires, yes, and many other types of aircraft, yet they had to make it Hurricanes!

He got a sergeant-pilot to run over the controls with him, and within seconds of his first take-off he was alone in a sky full of enemy planes. To add to his difficulties, his rear-view mirror was not adjusted, so he could not see over his tail. This meant that he had to do continuous steep turns with his head back to see what was coming after him. Moreover, he was wearing a borrowed helmet, much too big for him, and it kept slipping over his eyes. Then he could not find the switch to turn on his gunsight for a long time. All this while enemy machines were diving on him, yet somehow he held his own and finished by shooting down an Me109.

When he got back to the airfield to refuel, the ground crew told him that everyone had assumed that he must have been shot down. Ironically, after escapes of this sort, Howell was eventually wounded when he was on the ground during the airborne invasion of Crete. Tommy-gun slugs shattered his left shoulder and carried away part of his right forearm. An artery was severed, but comrades applied a tourniquet and went for a rescue party.

When the rescuers came, Howell was unconscious in a pool of blood. His right arm, from which the blood had come, lay across his stomach. He showed no sign of life. Assuming he had been hit in the stomach, they left him for dead. He would have been, he says, if he had had the strength to shoot himself, for in his fits of consciousness his sufferings were terrible.

The Germans found him eventually and he was flown to Greece. He endured months of agony, but British prisoner doctors saved his life. A day came when he was able to walk again, though both his arms were useless. It was while he lay awake one night, bemoaning his helplessness, embittered, bored with captivity, and near despair that an experience came to him which was to transform his life.

> . . . this was one of those nights when the mind takes control [he writes], and roves restlessly round. It carried me back through these long months in prison to days of battle and, beyond, to the wasted years before the war. It dwelt a moment there, long enough to see how selfish my life had been and to savour the despair of hopelessness about myself.
>
> It went back further and searched through childhood for the gleams of light which had illumined some of those days. Memories of laughter and of love, of the family and of home, were these intangibles to be lost for ever? Or was there something, just round the corner? I longed for home, the place where you loved and where your love was returned. I longed to be free—from prison, yes, but also from myself!

In this mood he recalled a day when his brother had returned home displaying a radiant happiness; a new kind of self-confidence. He had joined the Oxford Group! Howell, an atheist, had noted the change in his brother without desiring any such change in himself. He didn't want to have to alter his own way of life. It was easier

and more convenient to believe that there was no God,
though he was a son of the manse.

But his state of despair was such that there was nothing,
he says, that he was not prepared to do to be free. " What
if there was a God? " he asked himself. " Who could
make me different? Who could set me free? Who could
bring me home? Or bring home to me? At that
moment, God spoke to me. It was as though, by my
decision, I had switched on the light in a dark room."

He found himself praying, a thing he had not done for
ten years. He repeated the Lord's Prayer, and found that
it came not as a form of words but as an expression of
thought and feeling. He experienced ecstasy and shed
tears of joy. This, he says, continued for some time, and
was followed by utter peace and quiet. " I was sure and
secure in the belief that now I knew the secret of living."

Next day he was astounded to find that he was
" different." It had happened overnight. But the full
significance of what had happened to him did not strike
him till later. He had no time to be bored or sorry for
himself any more. He was fascinated by his new experience and added to it daily. " I found," he writes,
" that I could speak to God and be answered instantly."

In this new uplifted mood he felt a growing urge to
try and escape. He laid plans; got kit together, and took
some fellow prisoners into his confidence. No one
thought much of his chances. He was still very weak.
His left shoulder had almost healed, and the arm was stiff
and barely capable of being used for feeding and dressing
himself. Ten months' treatment had failed to heal his
right forearm, which was still open and discharging. It
was out of plaster, but swathed in bandages and useless.
The medical orderlies thought him crazy when he talked
about making a bid for freedom.

One evening, in bright moonlight, Howell decided to go.

He crossed the courtyard to a corner of the main wall, a spot he had previously reconnoitred. The top of the wall, covered with broken glass, was waist high, and he thought he might be able to swing a leg over. A couple of abortive attempts told him it was useless.

" In despair, I prayed to be shown what to do next," his story runs. " Should I go back? Or try elsewhere? " With that, his fear left him, and he realized that he could get over the wall without depending on his arms if he lay face downwards over it and wriggled his body round until he lay along it. Then he could drop down on the other side, feet first. He padded the broken glass with a mosquito net and some woollen things and leaned over them. The far side of the wall was in shadow. Trying to wriggle round, he overbalanced and pitched head first into the darkness.

And then a miracle.

> I found myself standing on the ground. I had fallen on my feet and was not even conscious of any jar to my arms as I landed. As I stood there, the padding which I had put over the broken glass fell into my hands. I did not even have to stoop to pick it up.

Standing in the shadow of tall houses, he listened to see if his escape had been noticed. There was no sign of pursuit, so he began to walk away, exulting in the thought that he was free.

Wondering which direction he should take, he decided to seek guidance.

> I referred to God and, even as I asked, I saw the star. It hung low in the sky and outshone every other star. Large and luminous, it was like a lamp on the distant horizon. Somehow I knew it. . . . I checked up on my bearings, finding the Plough and thence the Pole Star. My guiding star lay approximately in the East.

So he kept on, following his star, until he came to a little ravine. The moon was obscured now by clouds, and he found himself on the edge of a stream, unable to see.

But he felt he should step out blindly, trusting in the power which had so amazingly preserved him till then.

> My feet came down on hard stone with each step in the pitch darkness [he declares]. I found myself on the other side and my feet were not even wet. I must have trod on big stones near the surface.

And so the story runs, with the author seeking guidance whenever he feels at a loss. Thus:

> I decided that the situation was out of my control if indeed it had ever been in it. God must decide and tell me what to do.

He takes to the mountains, falls in with a little band of escaped Australian soldiers, and finally wins through to Turkey and safety. He is convinced that guidance brought him through.

Back in Cairo he found it impossible to recapture the careless irresponsibility of past days there.

> Then adventure had been to behave outrageously, to get drunk, to flirt and be foolish. Now, all that seemed empty and childish. I had tasted real adventure and the flavour of the old was sour.

Air Chief Marshal Tedder invited him to lunch to hear his story at first-hand and afterwards authorized his immediate return to England by air. And in London Howell retold his story at another luncheon party—at 10 Downing Street, as the guest of Sir Winston and Lady Churchill.

Yes; people *are* more important than things. I count my meeting with Loudon Hamilton and Edward Howell as of more than passing interest. They are men of two generations; both hard-headed Scots; both men of action. The one a soldier of World War I; the other an airman of World War II. The oldest convert to Buchmanism and one of the newest; key pieces, perhaps, in the puzzling picture I am striving to build.

A litter of other pieces lies waiting before me. There will be much head-scratching before my picture is complete.

CHAPTER 4

A Film to Change the World

MY encounter with Edward Howell had taken place just outside the entrance of Mountain House. I was waiting there to link up with a party which was going into Lausanne that afternoon to view some of the " rushes " from the film of *The Good Road*.

Dr Morris Martin had suggested that I might like to see them, for he remembered that I had watched a little of the actual filming during my casual visit in July. " You may be interested to see how it has come on since then," he said, and naturally I accepted the invitation at once. It opened up yet another avenue of inquiry in this many-sided mystery I was trying to probe. Every fresh scrap of data I could gather would be of value.

I knew that the Buchmanites were very proud of this enterprise and ranked this film as a powerful weapon to be wielded in the cause of Moral Re-Armament. It was something bigger than anything they had attempted so far in the way of popular propaganda. Through it they expected to reach new multitudes everywhere.

A great deal of money and effort had been sunk in it, and the intention was to secure world-wide distribution of the film—an elaboration of the stage show of the same name which had been presented on a free-admittance basis at His Majesty's Theatre, London, in 1948. Some London critics had ignored the production; others had been lukewarm in their comments; but it had caused more stir in America, having played on Broadway, in Boston, Los Angeles, and Washington. In the latter city, I was told, it had been seen by one-third of the members of both Houses of Congress during the critical debates on the Marshall Plan.

The revue had also been taken to Canada, where performances had been given in Ottawa and Montreal. It had toured the Western Zones of Germany at the invitation of Minister Presidents and Cabinet Ministers and, with the co-operation of General Clay, had been presented in Munich, Stuttgart, Frankfurt, Essen, and Dusseldorf.

It was estimated that a quarter of a million people had seen the show to date; but the film was to eclipse all this. Already, I was told, requests had come for copies to be prepared in fifteen languages. English, French, and German editions would have full spoken dialogue, while other languages would be featured in sub-titles.

All these details, and many more, I gleaned from James Coulter, who had been put in charge of the publicity. He explained that H. W. "Bunny" Austin, the former Davis Cup tennis star, had drafted the original outline for the revue. Then Alan Thornhill, Oxford Don and author of *The Forgotten Factor*, had collaborated with him in preparing the script of the film. Other Groupers had contributed ideas.

The party which set off for Lausanne to view the "rushes" was not a large one. We went in a cavalcade of half a dozen cars, and I found myself seated beside the secretary of the Oxford Group, Roland W. Wilson, with Mrs Wilson, Garth Lean, and James Coulter as the other passengers.

Our actual destination proved to be the Lausanne Palace Hotel (of which the Aga Khan is part owner), for arrangements had been made for the "rushes" to be shown in the private theatre there. It was small and very stuffy, and I was relieved when Dr Buchman, who was seated out at one side, as he had been at the morning's

Assembly, leapt up after the first strip had been run through and gave orders for the doors to be thrown open to let in some fresh air. He repeated his command between each " rush," and it was well he did, for during the longer sequences the atmosphere became almost unbearable.

There were two short sequences which I had seen filmed when visiting the improvised studio which the Buchmanites had built in the Comptoir Suisse—the local " Olympia." One, depicting the sealing of the Magna Carta, I had thought finely grouped and lit, so I was interested to see the " rush " and to pick out the familiar faces.

Ivan Menzies, Gilbert and Sullivan Opera star from Australia, as Bishop William of London; Edward A. Bell, former headmaster of St Bee's School, as Bishop Peter of Winchester; the Hon Miles B. W. Phillimore as Robert Fitzwalter, Mareschal of the Army of God and Holy Church. I had met them all in the studio. They, like all the other players, were giving their services; and expert technicians, who were there from Hollywood, were likewise working without fee. Co-directors were Edward H. Griffith and Howard Bretherton.

Griffith, who directed *One Night in Lisbon* and *Bahama Passage*, and Bretherton, who made *The Hills of Virginia*, with Rin Tin Tin, and, more recently, *Whispering Footsteps* for Warner Brothers, must have found it strange, I reflected, handling the Buchmanite players. As I watched the " rushes " now, I recalled how Griffith, after repeated retakes of one scene, had called out wearily: " Now, shall we all just have a ' quiet time '? " It was an inspiration, for after this brief relaxation, the tension broken, the scene was played as the director desired it.

At luncheon in the studios I had sat between Mr and Mrs Guy Pearce (formerly with Metro-Goldwyn-Mayer,

British), who were jointly responsible for make-up and hairdressing. They had come out of retirement to lend a hand, and Guy was itching to get back to British Columbia for the salmon-fishing.

" We're not MRA," his wife had confided to me during luncheon, " but we're lending a hand because we believe that they're good people. But, gee! I wish their women would use just a tiny *smeech* of lip-rouge. What a difference it would make! I suppose you know they don't use cosmetics? You'd never believe the job I had trying to get them to agree to wearing film make-up. I had to tell them ' you'll look just ghastly in the film if you don't '."

After that luncheon I had met some of the other technicians. The camera man, Richard Angst, who won an Academy Award with his documentary *Climbing the Matterhorn*, and whose *White Hell of Piz Palu* I had seen in an apt setting, in Switzerland, at a Wengen hotel. I also met David Forrest, chief sound engineer, who told me he was on special leave from Warner's. As their chief music engineer since 1936, he had handled musicals with such stars as Al Jolson, Joan Crawford, and Danny Kaye, but he was thoroughly enthusiastic about *The Good Road* film. His wife, another Hollywood expert, was the Buchmanites' assistant film editor.

It was quite clear from all this that the filming was being tackled in the same spirit as were all other Moral Re-Armament projects I had seen. Viewing the " rushes " now, I tried to assess its chances of success, making every allowance for their unedited state and the fact that background music was missing from certain sequences that were shown. Frankly, I thought those chances slim. The cast had worked hard, and it was obvious that they had enjoyed doing so; but there were crudities which the technicians from Hollywood, with all their necromancy, had been unable to overcome.

E

One brief sequence in which visionary glimpses of such characters as Washington, Lincoln, Jefferson, Joan of Arc, St Francis, and Keir Hardie were given, and in which each voiced an inspiring message, had possibilities. It was brilliantly photographed and the lines spoken had been well chosen; but the visions appeared to an oddly assorted set of people who a moment before had been arguing about " changing " Scotsmen and unlocking the wealth in English hearts.

The rest of the material seemed woefully thin, though the propaganda was interlarded thickly enough. A western farmyard setting, reminiscent in style of *Oklahoma*, served to introduce an incredible story of a feud between a farmer, Zeke, a crusty old bachelor, and his young neighbour, Rufe.

Rufe's cattle have broken Zeke's fences, so Zeke gets his gun and announces his determination to shoot Rufe immediately he shows up. But Rufe appears with his young wife hanging on his arm and bearing a spice cake she has baked specially to placate their rough neighbour! When Rufe says, " Sorry," and his wife holds out the spice cake, Zeke lays aside his gun, which is the cue for everyone to start singing:

> The whole world is my neighbour
> When you and I get together . . .

If this is a sample of the film that is going to change the world, I thought, the Buchmanites *must* be crazy. I couldn't believe that anyone could seriously advance such a preposterous story as offering a solution to world problems. By the same token the second world war could have been avoided if Chamberlain had taken a spice cake in his luggage when he went to meet Hitler.

*   *   *

Yet afterwards, when some of the Buchmanites pressed for my honest opinion of the rushes, they were quite

shocked that I hadn't been carried away by that scene.
"But it's based on real life!" they protested. "The
idea came from an incident between two neighbouring
farmers which took place in an area in Western Canada
known as 'Trouble Corner'." I felt like saying they
would be heading for trouble corner if that sequence
were left in the finished film; but I suddenly remembered
that I was their guest, and changed the subject.

Following this queer film show we adjourned for tea
on the hotel terrace—a treat, I was told, arranged by Dr
Buchman himself. I found myself seated at a small table
with the Rt Reverend George West, the Lord Bishop
of Rangoon, to whom I had been introduced earlier
as "a man who asks very penetrating questions." He
gave me a genial smile and whispered: "Ah! now's your
chance to cross-examine me!" At least, I thought he was
whispering, but it turned out that he was suffering from
a relaxed throat. In the circumstances I decided to spare
him. I had no special questions to ask him, anyway.

Instead he began to question me. How long had I been
in my profession? What sort of articles did I write?
How was it that I came to be making this inquiry into
Moral Re-Armament? It was a change to be answering
questions instead of putting them, but conversation was
almost impossible, for our table was on the edge of the
dance-floor and the band was blaring away behind us.

In that incongruous setting, then, while sophisticated
couples swished past, dancing cheek-to-cheek, the Lord
Bishop battled bravely against the dual handicap of his
relaxed throat and the strident music, to tell me that
Moral Re-Armament was firmly established in Burma. It
was an unequal contest, and I was glad for his sake when
the music stopped.

He gave me an International Souvenir copy of the
Burman, which I found to be full of articles dealing with

Moral Re-Armament, including one he had written under the heading: " The Ideology of Change." In it he told an anecdote which yielded the best and most concise summary of Buchmanite ideology I had yet encountered. Here it is:

> A man, while working at his desk, was being bothered by his little boy. A map of the world was lying on his table. He tore it into pieces and threw it on the floor.
> " Now then," he said. " Try putting that together."
> In a short space the boy was back with the map. The father was surprised. " How did you manage to do that so quickly? "
> " It was easy, Father," he said, " because I found on the other side of the map there was a picture of a man, and I found that when the man came right, the world came right."

There you have the essence of Dr Buchman's teaching, a teaching which probably derives from his own Eastern travels. Change people and the world will change, he argues. He holds, with Confucius, that moral order must precede political order.

Were I a Buchmanite I would probably say that I was " guided " to the Bishop's table that afternoon. Anyway, the meeting was propitious. One more piece of the jig-saw had slipped into place.

On the drive back to Mountain House I again sat beside the Oxford Group's secretary, Roland Whitwell Wilson, MA, and seized the opportunity to bombard him with questions. He bore the onslaught good-naturedly, though I gave him no respite. As soon as he had disposed of one point to my satisfaction, I fired another poser at him. He impressed me as being utterly sincere and a man of high integrity.

Perhaps it was taking an unfair advantage of him, for he was driving and the road was a busy one. But I felt that the opportunity might not present itself again. Although I was not yet through my first day, I had seen enough of the routine at Mountain House to realize that there was very little prospect of being able to get anyone alone. My interview with Loudon Hamilton had been conducted under difficulty, for there had been about four other people at our table, and Hamilton's narrative had been delivered piecemeal between snatches of general conversation.

So I became quite relentless in pestering the secretary for information, and by dint of my persistence succeeded in disposing of dozens of points. In the end he had become so used to answering questions that he even began to disclose facts for which I had not asked. For instance, he volunteered the information that the car he was driving, a big saloon, had been given to him. It was a present, he declared, from someone who had " been changed in rather a wonderful way."

I was so surprised by this gratuitous revelation that I didn't think of asking who that someone was or in what circumstances the " change " had taken place. But later I gathered that it was quite a commonplace for wealthy converts to reward the Buchmanite who had been instrumental in effecting their conversion.

Instead of setting forth a string of queries and answers as they were put and received during that ride between Lausanne and Caux, it will be better to summarize them under specific headings.

Thus, on the subject of expenses, I learned that these were voted by the Finance Committee, but that the Committee was not empowered to vote expenses for its own members. I gathered, also, that there was no bar to any Buchmanite accepting cash donations as individual " presents." Many full-time workers were, in fact, living on money they obtained from people who felt prompted to support them in their work.

In connection with the flood of goods of all kinds which had poured into Mountain House I had noted that these were always listed as from Canada, Holland, Denmark, and so on. This, I found, did not mean that they were gifts from the Governments of the countries named, but from rich industrialists within those countries who were sympathetic towards the cause of Moral Re-Armament. Sometimes these gifts had been solicited by the Buchmanites.

I was interested, too, in the organization of " Task Forces," which were always being sent to different areas. One such force had been through Germany on a prolonged tour, giving performances of propaganda plays. I wanted to know how such ambitious campaigns were planned and financed.

The answer was that an advance guard usually went ahead to pave the way, get local authorities interested, arrange publicity, and perhaps fix up free accommodation in the home of sympathizers. Expenses would be voted for the campaign and a treasurer would accompany the task force to pay all incidental expenses as they might arise.

On this trip, too, I also gleaned some additional facts concerning the London headquarters. Apart from a mansion in Berkeley Square which admirers had presented to Dr Buchman, and the offices in Hays Mews, there were about five houses in Charles Street either owned by or loaned to members of the Oxford Group.

From my own observation I had noted that meals of different grade were served to various sections of guests at Mountain House. I now learned that there were three distinct services: one for invalids or others who might be on a special diet; the cafeteria service; and " the little dining-room."

A room was set aside for guests in the first category, and they had only to specify their particular needs for them to be met. The cafeteria was, of course, the general service available to anyone. The " little dining-room "

was able to provide limited service for senior Buchmanites
who had business to discuss or who wished to entertain
distinguished visitors.

Finally, I gathered that the Buchmanites were short of
Swiss currency. It made things " difficult," but they tried
to overcome it by settling as many items as possible in
London. Coaches chartered to meet planes at Geneva
were paid for in London, which helped to ease the
currency problem a little. Presently we stopped for
petrol and oil. The secretary of the Oxford Group, con-
fessing himself to be without francs, tried to coax Lean into
paying; but, weakly, I came to the rescue and handed
him the money. Somehow, I felt he had earned it.

*   *   *

That night, visiting the well-equipped theatre at
Mountain House, I sat through the stage version of *The
Good Road* revue. Lean had contrived to secure an odd
ticket, and as he handed it to me after dinner he explained
that they were in great demand and difficult to obtain.

" I've seen the show many times, of course," he told
me. " I advise you to get in early. Accommodation is
limited and the seats are soon snapped up."

There were 1,200 delegates at Mountain House, and
I suppose the theatre held less than half that number.
I never quite grasped the system by which tickets were
allocated, but I noticed that there appeared to be a lively
traffic in them. Numerous Buchmanites were to be seen
dashing about canvassing among their fellows to find
whether they had any surplus tickets for disposal.

Some, I saw, had a fistful of the coveted admittance
slips, which confirmed what I had already surmised from
observation—that there is a definite " know-how " at
Caux. Those who had the secret, it seemed, could pull
any strings successfully. They could not only reserve the
best seats in the theatre, but could always be sure of a

comfortable armchair seat in the main hall for the Assemblies.

Then, instead of joining the long queue for the cafeteria, those in the know were usually able to reserve a table in the " little dining-room," where superior meals were served in much greater comfort.　Could this, I wondered, be what the Buchmanites meant when they talked about " inspired democracy "?

Anyway, I strolled into the theatre early and made for a side seat, thinking that it would be convenient if I grew bored and wanted to leave.　After what I had seen in some of the " rushes " that afternoon, I was not particularly thrilled at the prospect of having to sit through the full stage show.

As I dropped into my self-chosen place a familiar voice greeted me.　In the next seat was my travelling companion of the preceding day—Mr Thomas Powell!　By some incalculable chance I had gone straight to his side in a hall in which there were scores of vacant places.

" It seems we can't get away from each other for long," I said.　" What sort of time have you been having? "

" Wonderful! " he exclaimed with enthusiasm.　" And you? "

I told him vaguely that I had been very well looked after, and he said he had, too.　The whole organization at Caux had been a revelation to him.　He had never expected to find anything like it.　But we were unable to compare notes further because the music, from the sound track of the film, started up at that moment.　The general buzz of conversation faded away as the lights were dimmed.　A quick glance round showed me that all the seats had filled.　The footlights glowed and the curtain rose upon the opening scene. . . .

In strict fairness I must set down the fact that the live show made a more favourable impression than the film

" rushes " had done. It was brightly dressed, well staged, and played with such tremendous zest by a youthful cast, that it would have been churlish not to have shown appreciation. It certainly " got across " with the audience, whose applause for every item was almost prodigal.

The music—there are about thirteen songs running through the revue—was cheerful and distinctive. Inquiring about it afterwards I found it had been recorded by the Suisse Romande Orchestra under the Buchmanite's own conductor, Dr William Reed.

A team of ten musicians—from America, Canada, England, Scotland, Denmark, Sweden, and France, had provided the score. The theme song, *The Good Road*, was the work of M. Paul Misraki, and, sung by an advancing mass of people in costumes of all nations against a huge illuminated globe of the world, it was most effective.

But many of the songs, though tuneful enough, were naïve attempts to put over uplift in the vein of Ella Wheeler Wilcox. I don't know what visiting statesmen and politicians made of them all, but the Buchmanites, at any rate, seemed to be whipped into ecstasy by such items as *Sorry is a Magic Little Word* or *If You Harnessed All the Heart-power in the World*.

I found it quite impossible to revise my estimate of the film. Much of it was sorry stuff, strung together in a haphazard sort of way, with the MRA propaganda laid on crudely. This puzzled me considerably, for I had studied enough examples of Buchmanite propaganda to know that they can be subtle enough when they choose.

Once more I yawned over the incredible sob-story of the tough feudist whose thoughts were diverted from neighbourcide by the gift of a spice cake; but there were other sketches just as callow. There was an American family scene, for instance, which opened with glimpses of father, mother, sister, brother, and grandma all preoccupied with their own selfish pursuits, constantly bickering.

The curtain fell, to rise again on a " changed " family, though how they had all become transformed we were not told. Now, of course, everyone was polite and kindly and the family was united. So united that they insisted upon singing two songs together—*Families Can Be Fun* and *Sorry is a Magic Little Word*. This last song was supposed, apparently, to provide a key to the whole sketch and a message of world importance. Learn to say " sorry," and harmony flies into the home ! And if that works in families, why not in the great family of nations?

Then came an industrial scene devised to show Moral Re-Armament as a bridge between Management and Labour. A stylized setting of giant cog-wheels, reminiscent of Chaplin's *Modern Times*, formed the background against which Management and Labour faced each other from opposite sides of the stage.

As the curtains rose on this scene the wheels of industry were turning smoothly, with groups of workers in American style overalls swaying in the background to simulate the rhythmic beat of pistons. Production was booming and both Management and Labour announced to the Press their intention of playing their full part in saving Democracy.

Then, for no apparent reason, a young minx named " Miss Trust " tripped in and gaily distributed little packets all round. She was sowing seeds of dissension between Management and Labour ! At this point my erstwhile strike-leader friend nudged me in the ribs and whispered : " Do you suppose it's a coincidence that she's dressed like that? "

For Miss Trust, " essence of subversion," was dressed wholly in red—a red hat, a red costume, and she carried a red handbag and a red umbrella.

Slowly the wheels of industry came to a stop, but just as Miss Trust began to wave her umbrella aloft and to laugh in triumph, a stranger strode on to the stage. A fine, upright fellow known, apparently as " Change." Holding the centre of the stage, he proceeded to give both Management and Labour a verbal injection of Moral Re-Armament ideology. So they united to throw " Miss Trust " out (having found her seed packets to be empty!), and the curtain fell on the wheels of industry turning once more. Oh! And I had almost forgotten it! Everybody singing: " There's enough in the world for everyone's need; but not for everyone's greed."

That fantastic scene ended the first half of the revue. The second half at least evinced more cohesion, since one main thread now ran through every scene. It turned out to be a kind of up-to-date *Pilgrim's Progress* depicting the passage of " Mr Anyman " through a wicked world.

An opening scene showed a " cabinet meeting " among organized forces of evil plotting to ensnare the people of the world. In the chair was a satanic personality called Materialism. Gathered about him were characters such as pride, greed, hate, fear, confusion, and lust. Their reports failed to satisfy him.

" What about Anyman—the most important man in the world? " he thundered. " Win him, and you win every-thing."

To trap " Mr Anyman " they transformed their board table into a semblance of an ultra-modern cocktail bar. And on his entry they fawned upon him, flattered him, pressed drink upon him. " Madame Lust " looked so seductive in the half light that I was sure he was going to fall! But his better self prevailed, apparently, and he rushed headlong from temptation to find himself, in the next scene, on a lonely hillside road.

Of course, you've guessed it! It was *The Good Road.*

But to avoid any misconceptions, a kindly old road-mender was on hand to explain. Besides being a road-mender, the yokel also proved to be something of a philosopher and poet.

" It runs right around the world," he said, describing the road. " Through little white villages and charred ruined towns, through the dust of ancient civilizations, through teeming cities, probably right past your own front door."

Then came the scene I had viewed in the film " rushes " —the encounter with an English girl, a Scotsman, and a Welsh miner, with an inconsequential argument about the wealth of English hearts, and Liberty. Mr Anyman, now revealed as an American, thought he knew all about Liberty, but the Scot disabused him.

" Listen, laddie," he said. " Where d'ye suppose your idea of liberty came from? "

" Aye," chimed in the road-mender. " Hast ever heard of Magna Carta? "

That was the cue for the vision of Runnymede to appear in the background, to be followed by visions of Joan of Arc, St Francis, Keir Hardie, and the rest! Then, without warning, these inspiring scenes faded, the lights went up, and a surging crowd of young people of all nations came trooping upon the stage singing: " Come along, it's an invitation, Mr Anyman! " They urged him to join them on the Good Road.

The smiling, happy band of international pilgrims converged upon Mr Anyman. Would he " change " and join them? Would he? That served to introduce another song:

What are you going to do, Mister,
  Where do you go from here?
  The world will soon wake up and take your cue,
What are you going to do, Mister?
  It's up to you.

They left him to decide, and he saw another vision—that of a soldier in battle kit. The phantom spoke: "Stand beside me, friend, while you can still fight to make our dreams come true. Stand beside me, or millions will lie beside me in the years to come."

The figure dissolved, to be replaced by a white cross. Mr Anyman's mind was made up. He would march with the throng. People of all nations filled the stage and, with Mr Anyman in their midst, gave a final rendering of their theme song, *The Good Road*, as the curtain slowly fell.

It is perhaps idle to attempt a serious criticism of such a show, with its moments of bathos and banality interspersed with a lot of competent stagecraft and some really tuneful music. For me the one redeeming feature was the ecstatic gusto of the players. It was evident that they believed their show to be an inspired creation. They had enjoyed every second of it.

Someone had told me that it was the tradition with MRA shows for the audience to flock on to the stage afterwards and mingle with the players. But I had had enough. My day had been a singularly full one, so I slipped away to my room to try to sort out the multiple impressions which were buzzing through my brain.

Some aspects of the day's investigations were so incongruous that I found them baffling. On the one hand I had met many people of quite outstanding character and attainments—successful men of the world, distinguished scholars, prominent churchmen, men of great talent, men of great charm, travelled men, and men of action. They had left me in no doubt as to their sincerity—and yet . . .

How was the presence of such people at Caux to be reconciled with the commonplace assembly I had attended that morning? How could they give up their valuable time to sit through such a puerile propaganda show as I had just witnessed? Could they possibly imagine that these demonstrations were making an important contribution towards the solution of world problems?

Could they honestly accept the Buchmanites' own valuation and bring themselves to believe that this kind of parlour-charade evangelism presented " an unrivalled opportunity to create and strengthen the ideological links between nations upon which the unity of Europe and the future of civilization depends "?

Did any of them seriously believe that world strife could be averted by a team of jolly teenagers chorusing *Sorry is a Magic Little Word*? Or did they think that warmongering nations could be appeased with spice cake?

Against these thoughts I weighed evidence I had seen of superb organizing ability on the part of the Buchmanites. I thought of the tremendous zeal with which they tackled every part of their queer programme. I thought of their prodigal expenditure and of the dazzling façade they presented to the world.

At about that juncture my room-mate came in. He looked exhausted. Undressing, almost in silence, he threw himself into bed with a great, heaving sigh.

" I've just done four hours' washing dishes! " he explained as he bade me good night.

And, of course, that set me thinking again. Was I being unfair to these Buchmanites, who followed their chosen way of life with an almost fanatical zeal? Was I wasting my time trying to balance a lot of incongruous impressions? Was I unusually dull? Was there something I had missed? Something yet to be revealed, perhaps, that would explain why so many distinguished people had deemed it worth while to come to Caux? I didn't know. But I felt impelled to go on probing until I had the answer.

CHAPTER 5

Catching Them Young

" GIVE me a child for the first seven years," runs an old maxim attributed to the Jesuits, " and you may do what you like with him afterwards." Ever since the day in 1921 when Dr Buchman descended upon Oxford to cast his net among the undergraduates, he has shown especial interest in young converts.

On my arrival at Caux I had expressed a wish to meet as many cross-sections of the Oxford Group's adherents as possible during my stay, and on my second evening, before visiting the theatre as described in the last chapter, I dined with a number of young Buchmanites.

Lean had organized the dinner on my behalf, so I suppose the guests were all aware that they were to act as my " guinea-pigs." It meant an extra-special meal in " the little dining-room " for them, and they came to table in sparkling mood, eager enough to talk or to " testify."

All were very self-assured. Their ages ranged from about sixteen to twenty-seven. Even the youngest members had poise and polish.

They were all students in the " College of the Good Road," recently established by the Buchmanites for the purpose of imparting ideological training to sons and daughters of their followers. With them came their tutor, Mr Roger Hicks, author of *How to Read the Bible*—a best-seller in the Buchmanite bookshop.

He sat at my right hand and introduced his pupils to me in turn. After I had explained the purpose of my visit to Caux, I invited them to tell me something about themselves. Working clockwise round the table, I got potted biographies from each, then we plunged into general discussion.

It was impossible not to like those youngsters. They represented contrasting types, yet they had in common an intelligent interest in world affairs and an urge to play an active part in moulding the shape of things to come. They were not prigs. Nor were they too serious-minded. Those with whom I dined showed a sense of humour and were wholly natural. They certainly made a good impression upon me.

There was Daniel Mottu, for example, whose elder brother, Philippe Mottu, is President of the Fondation du Réarmement Morale. He told me he was twenty-seven and had studied at Geneva University, where he had taken a law degree. While there he had been president of the leading student society and had developed an interest in international affairs.

Born in Geneva, son of a Calvinist clergyman, and youngest of a family of seven, he had taken part in the bell-ringing celebrations at the laying of the foundation stone of the Palace of the League of Nations. The hopes the world had pinned upon it had been shattered before he was out of his teens.

His introduction to Moral Re-Armament had come through his elder brother. He had attended the 1946 Assembly at Caux, and it had made a lasting impression upon him. He secured his law degree in the following year and also began to contribute articles on political and ideological topics to the *Journal de Genève*.

Then he decided to throw in his lot with the Buchmanites and travelled with *The Good Road* show in America, Canada, and Germany. After being in London for the performance at His Majesty's Theatre, he returned to Switzerland for his Army service. Now, with his brother and mother, he is giving all his time to Moral Re-Arma-

Delegates to the World Assembly for Moral Re-Armament (left to right, *Dr E. Yalman, Turkey ; Senator Francisco Gallotti, Brazil ; Jun Murai, Japan*) *meet outside the London home of Dr Buchman, and once that of Clive of India.*

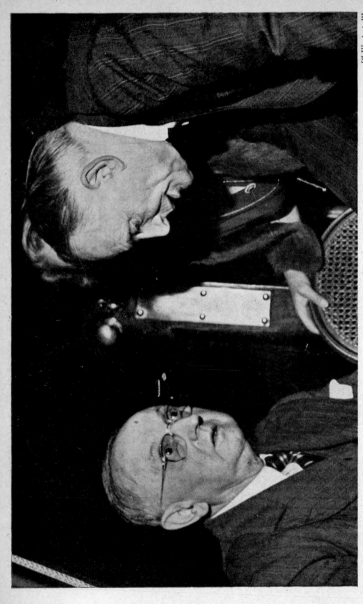

Dr Buchman confers with Sir Roy Pinsent during a rehearsal of the Moral Re-Armament revue, The Good Road

ment. He helped to prepare the 1949 Assembly at Caux, and is co-editor of an information bulletin which is issued weekly during the sessions. He is now studying in the College of the Good Road.

One of his fellow students with whom I also chatted was Richard Channer, son of Major-General Channer. A " veteran " of the campaign in Burma, where he was wounded and gained the MC, and with six years' Army service behind him, this young man is ready to fight for the Buchmanite ideology for the rest of his days. His father has been associated with the movement for many years.

Other youngsters I met at Caux included Anida K. Sinha, youngest son of Lord Sinha, only Indian peer in the House of Lords. He is now supplementing the education he received at Charterhouse by studying in the College of the Good Road. Then there was Gordon Wise, son of the former Prime Minister of Western Australia. Practical minded, and with a record of three years in the Royal Australian Air Force, he, too, believes wholeheartedly in the gospel of Moral Re-Armament.

I also met a young Finn, Klaus Snellman, who not only assured me of his faith in the movement, but added that two of his brothers were in it, too.

Among the girl students at the College of the Good Road I have already mentioned the two daughters of Colonel Hore-Ruthven, of the Black Watch, who played hostess on the night of my arrival at Mountain House. The three daughters of Lady Rennell of Rodd are also undergoing this ideological training.

Here is a typical testimony of one young woman student, Christine Nowell, of Cheshire, who has the role of the English girl in *The Good Road* revue. Having seen her on the stage and in the film studio at Lausanne, I was naturally interested to learn her views.

F

" Money, dates, society, and independence," she has said, " were the false gods of my life. I used to think that my career in the theatre [she was training for ballet] would fulfil all of these. I prided myself on being sophisticated and superior—and on being able to hide what really went on inside. When a person like this meets people who are real, unaffected, and honest with you about themselves, something is bound to happen. I began to see myself as I really was. I saw that a girl can either use the gifts God has given her to destroy moral standards—or she can use them to build the kind of atmosphere in which men can do the creative thinking which the world most needs today."

Christine Nowell is twenty-four. Not all the young Buchmanites are quite so intense. She had taken part in the first post-war International Ballet Festival at Copenhagen and had had three years' experience on the ballet stage when she decided to throw it all up in favour of Buchmanism.

" I have found that the theatre, instead of being a setting in which I could shine," she declared, " could become a beacon light to transform and guide the thinking of people across the world."

Students, I found, were being drawn from all countries. The Government of East Indonesia was sending six specially chosen young men. The President's son, Parsi Soekawati, was already there, and had completed six months of study.

Dr Chen Li-fu, Chinese Cabinet Minister, had arranged for six Chinese boys to train at Caux; and Dr B. C. Roy, Vice-Chancellor of Calcutta University, was likewise sending a batch of Indian students.

There were youngsters from America, youngsters from Japan, from Norway, from Italy, from Sweden, Germany, Canada, Czechoslovakia, Eire, and Denmark. Many of these, I was told, had graduated in universities in their own countries and were undergoing post-graduate courses at the College of the Good Road.

Thus, a completely new field of inquiry presented itself. The implications of this widespread scheme for pressing young minds into the Buchmanite mould were so immense that I realized that the venture could not be dismissed as just another offshoot of an already formidable organization.

So I pressed for further details of the College itself, and was handed a very handsome brochure in which, it was said, I would find all the information I could possibly need. At the same time it was impressed upon me that fees quoted—£600 for a year's training—might be subject to revision. The whole brochure was, in fact, at present under review by leading Buchmanites, and it was quite possible that the scheme might be modified or amplified should it not meet with their unanimous approval.

Printed in Switzerland, this prospectus had been most lavishly produced. Anyone handling it, I felt, could hardly fail to be impressed.

Names that were beginning to grow familiar leapt to my eye among the list of the Board of Governors. Edward A. Bell, MA (Oxon), whom I had last seen playing Bishop Peter of Winchester in *The Good Road* film, headed the list. And a few lines below was the Hon. Miles G. W. Phillimore, who had played " Robert Fitzwalter " in the Magna Carta scene.

Next came the name of my invisible host, Sir Roy Pinsent, Bt, BA (Oxon), solicitor, whose own daughter, Rosemary, was a student in the College. The Oxford Group's secretary, Roland W. Wilson, MA (Oxon), was also on the Board; so was Alan Thornhill, MA (Oxon), formerly Fellow, Hertford College, Oxford; so was the Rev Julian Thornton-Duesbery, MA (Oxon), Principal, Wycliffe Hall, Oxford.

Then there were other names, unfamiliar to me at the moment, though some of them were to crop up again before my inquiries were concluded. There was Bernard M. Hallward, BA (Oxon), President of St Raymond Paper Ltd, Canada; and George Marjoribanks, MA (Edin.), BSc, BD; and Philip R. Peters, BA (Cantab), MRCS, LRCP; and Miss Irene Prestwich, Tirley Garth, Tarporley, Cheshire; and Garrett R. Stearly, BA (Yale), BD.

I turned the page to be greeted by seventy-two miniature portraits of smiling young men and women—" some students of the College of the Good Road." Facing this galaxy of smiles were three quotations. The first, from Plato, said:

> The noblest of all studies is the study of what man should be and how he should live.

The next was from Lecomte du Nouy in *Human Destiny*:

> The time has come for nations, as well as individuals, to know what they want. . . . It is only by direct action on youth that a better society can be successfully moulded. . . . Can we not find leaders of sufficient vision to conceive an international plan of moral development spreading over generations, instead of economic plans of five years? It would be a magnificent task.

And finally, bearing the date May 26, 1949, were these words of HRH the Princess Elizabeth:

> It would be the greatest service to mankind if the British peoples . . . should be the pioneers of a moral and spiritual revival without which all their great material achievements will have been in vain.

In the pages which followed, the aims and objects of the College were set forth at great length and cleverly backed up by numerous illustrations. "Sandhurst, St Cyr, and West Point were founded to provide officers for the war of arms," I read. " The College of the Good Road is being founded to provide officers in the war of ideas, men and women morally and spiritually sound and clear, and fully trained in ideology."

The need for such a college was said to be imperative. Alien ideologies, it was pointed out, had had a long start, and had largely succeeded in confusing and capturing the minds and morals of youth in college and industry across the world.

"Today," the prospectus went on, " Communist China is but one of the countries being run by those trained twenty years ago in ideological schools in Moscow."

The founding of the College of the Good Road, then, was held to be " an answering development in line with the movement of history." Every great advance in education, it was argued, had been designed for a special purpose. Universities of the Middle Ages had been specifically concerned with training men for the ministry and tasks of government and law which clergy of those days normally performed.

Then, in the nineteenth century, the Industrial Revolution created a need to equip men technically for a mechanical and scientific age. At the same time, Arnold's education in the British Public School was designed to create wise captains of industry and administrators of Empire.

" The founding of the College of the Good Road marks a third phase," the prospectus argued, " this time in response to the needs of the ideological age. Its aim is to turn out officer-statesmen in the war of ideas, equipped with an answering ideology based on absolute moral standards and the guidance of God."

The prospectus ran to sixty-five pages, but I persevered, and studied it closely, so as to make quite sure of missing nothing.

I gathered that training of the kind it was proposed to

give in the College had been tried out in practice over a period of four years with pupils drawn from twenty-five nations. Several hundred youths had been trained continuously, it was claimed, by " travelling in more than one country with the forces of Moral Re-Armament."

> They have attended lectures, written essays, and taken part in tutorial groups. They have met and talked with ordinary men and leaders in every section of a nation's life; lived in the homes of workers, industrialists, labour leaders, and politicians. They have visited factories, local governments, parliaments, and newspaper offices. They have spoken at Rotary Clubs, Chambers of Commerce, Trade Union meetings, in factories, in schools and colleges, and over the air. They have prepared and given ideological training courses to thousands of youth, as well as to adults; *they have gained rich experience in writing, composing, and producing the musical revue, " The Good Road," and other weapons in the war of ideas.*

The italics are mine. All roads, it seemed, were to lead back to *The Good Road* revue.

* * *

Still, I didn't discard the brochure on that account. I wanted to find out something about the curriculum. This, I learned farther on, was not as haphazard as the preceding passages had suggested.

First among the listed subjects, appropriately enough, came History; but, reading on, I found that it was history with a difference—" a moral and spiritual interpretation " of the subject. There were to be lectures on the materialistic interpretation which " provides the basis for the Communist ideology, and to which the course provides the answer."

Second subject in the syllabus was Psychology. " The understanding of people and of relationships in home, industry, and nation," it was claimed, would be " taught by men and women who know: (1) that human nature can be changed, because that change has taken place in themselves, and (2) that God can guide, because they daily experience His direction."

Psychology so taught, it was said, ceased to be an endless study of problems, and became a study of the answer to problems and of the art of liberating the best creative resources in the human personality for the task of remaking the world.

Then came Economics—the Buchmanite idea of Economics, that is, with the announcement that students would be taught to live and to articulate

> the new economy where *Give* is the primary motive instead of *Get*; where everyone cares enough and everyone shares enough so that everyone may have enough; where the wealth of the world is made available for all and for the exploitation of none; where ownership involves stewardship. Students are trained to live and give the answer alike to the casual materialism of the ordinary man in every class and country and to the calculated economic determinism of the Marxist.

Under the heading " Government," it was explained that courses were given dealing specially with the history and foundations of democracy. And—" students also have opportunities of meeting leaders of local and national governments."

" Industrial Leadership " was given as the next subject to be tackled. Experts would lecture on the management and the labour side in such subjects as the history of trade unionism in different countries; the true function of management; the ideological struggle within labour and within management; industrial incentives; industrial relations, and industrial democracy. Students would be enabled to study particular industries and factories at first hand and to take part in industrial round-table conferences.

Under the subject " Languages " it was stated that students would be trained to become proficient in at least one language other than their mother tongue.

"Writing" would involve periodic essays set by the tutors; but students would be encouraged and "taught" how to be correspondents for their home newspapers, besides being trained in "the interpretation of news and the preparation of articles." Selected students would receive special training in the editing of periodicals such as the Buchmanite's propaganda magazine *New World News*, and in the preparation of books and pamphlets for publication.

As might be expected, "Public Speaking" was included in this ambitious syllabus. Students, it said, would be trained in the planning of meetings, studying how to present "the truth each has to offer"—in terms the modern man could understand. "From a first hard-won utterance of a few sentences," it was claimed, "many a student has progressed until he is addressing large assemblies. One young man, a Labour leader's son, aged nineteen, spoke effectively before 70,000 people in the course of a single year. Others have prepared and presented radio programmes."

"Drama" came next with an intimation that students would be trained to understand the function of drama as a primary ideological weapon. They would be given an opportunity to take part, front or backstage, "in such productions as *The Good Road* and *The Forgotten Factor*, and in films."

"Music." Teaching would be given in the history of music, "with special reference to its ideological interpretation; in musical appreciation; in the study of music as an ideological weapon today; and in the creation and use of positive musical weapons in the war of ideas." Selected individuals would be specially trained in vocal and instrumental technique, composition, conducting, publishing, radio, and film music.

Finally, came "Domestic Economy." It was explained

that students would live during their course in the homes of workers and industrialists and in specially selected homes where Moral Re-Armament is the basis of family life. " This gives them an intimate understanding of the life and culture of nations in which they are studying."

Women would be given special training in all the domestic arts: cooking, housekeeping, home management, and the care of children. Both men and women would be shown how " to make administration, catering and household tasks part of the basic training in democratic living."

A separate section of the brochure was devoted to a review of work accomplished by existing students of the College of the Good Road during the first three months of 1949. It was prefaced by the following remarks, taken, it was proudly announced, from a report by an actual student:

> 1949 is a fateful year. The word "ideology" has become as common in newsprint as whisky ads. and divorces. The cold war has become a hot reality in the minds of ordinary people. And the need for an answer has forced itself upon nation after nation.
>
> A year in the College of the Good Road has taken us through many countries. Our classrooms have been in mines, factories, drawing rooms, lecture halls and parliaments; our professors and teachers have been labour leaders, business men and statesmen. Our fellow-students have come from twenty-five different nations, from homes rich and poor, and every possible background.
>
> In travelling, learning and working together, we have found the answer which we are being trained to give the world, to be simple and always valid.

Their studies, apparently, took twenty-six of them " up grain elevators " in Liverpool, " down mines " in Doncaster, " through tanneries " in Runcorn, and to steel works and textile factories. Ten others went to France, to visit the Louvre, Notre Dame, and the Tuileries, and to watch proceedings in the Chamber of Deputies. They toured some of France's richest farming country; they lived with French families; visited the battlefields of World War I; saw chemical plants; stayed in Lille; lunched with the Mayor of Lens.

Meanwhile another group went with *The Forgotten Factor* on a tour through eighteen German cities; lived in German homes; participated in trade union meetings in the British, American, and French zones, and had conferences with their youth leaders. This same group visited the universities of Tübingen, Freiburg, Heidelberg, and Mainz.

Yet another class spent the three months in South Wales, living in the homes of miners and steelworkers throughout the Rhondda Valley. Others went to the Scandinavian countries, others to Scotland and Holland. They visited cultural centres or inspected local industries.

Accompanying this record of the students' activities were numerous photographs showing them at work on their unorthodox "lessons." Some lined up on skis in Norwegian snowfields; others singing on the Stockholm radio; others being fêted in Holland. What youngster would not be thrilled at the prospect of joining a "College" which offered such alluring opportunities?

* * *

A third section of the brochure, I found, dealt with permanent training centres in various parts of the world. There was one, known as "The Club," at Los Angeles, California; another on Mackinac Island, Michigan; one in England, at Tarporley, Cheshire.

A fourth section gave portraits of "some of the 300 students from twenty nations" who were said to be devoting their full time to training for the war of ideas. These included Yori and Naoko Mitsui, from Japan, whose father was described as "Chairman of the Board of Directors of the Mitsui Educational Foundation." There was also Kirsti Hakkarainen, a factory girl from Finland, said to have twice lost her home and all her possessions in the wars with Russia. There was Peter Petersen, from Germany, said to have been trained in Nazism from the age of eight, and quoted as declaring the ideology of the College of the Good Road to be superior for four reasons. First, because it has given him and his nation absolute moral standards instead of relative standards; next, because it is not dependent on one man; again, because it is for everyone everywhere, and not limited to one race, class, or nation; and, finally, because it rests not in a dictator or party, but in the guidance of God.

Page after page of smiling portraits of young people from Canada, America, Holland, Sweden, Italy, Belgium, and many other countries, helped to foster the impression that the College of the Good Road must be the jolliest institution ever founded.

But even this did not complete the brochure. A fifth section was devoted to essays contributed by students who had completed three months' work. A Canadian student wrote:

> Can I give to a Communist the superior idea of teamwork as opposed to class warfare? Yes, I've been at college, the College of the Good Road. . . .

A Swiss wrote:

> In Hamburg word reached some of us that we had immediately to come down to Switzerland to help in the production of the movie of *The Good Road*. The frontline in the war of ideas can be just as much in a movie studio as in a union hall or executive office in the Ruhr.

A young Dane wrote:

> Facing the tough realities in South Wales, we had to live our ideology during twenty-four hours a day. . . .

For all their smiling faces, these youngsters take

themselves very seriously. It is evident that they have been steeped in Buchmanite doctrines until they are quite incapable of thinking for themselves. As missionaries, they will work with an almost fanatical zeal wherever they are sent. That, of course, is precisely what Dr Buchman desires. When someone once said to him that the world needed a new John Wesley, he retorted: " What about a lot of little Wesleys? "

Hence the College of the Good Road, and the other training centres which he has already established. Still more colleges are planned in different countries, all to be linked together by an international committee. Each country will have its own governing body and its representatives on the international advisory committee.

It has all been worked out to the smallest detail, apparently. The international committee is to consist not only of eminent educators but also of leaders from all branches of national life.

While lectures and tutorial classes were to be a definite part of the education provided by the College, much important knowledge and training would be gained, it was said, from practical experience, by travelling and working with those already trained in the war of ideas. In fact, the College of the Good Road was described as " peripatetic rather than residential."

I saw now why so many student leaders had been invited to Caux for the present session, and I made it my business to obtain a list of these. It was interesting. Britain was most strongly represented by about ten student delegates, including a Don from Bristol University, a Rhodes Scholar and Double Blue from Oxford, the President of Nottingham University students, and the President of Birmingham University students.

Czechoslovakia had triple representation in the President of Czech students in Switzerland, a member of the

Committee of Union for all Czech students in exile, and the Secretary of Czech students in England.

Art students of Berlin had sent their Chairman; Bavarian students had sent their Vice-President; Heidelberg students their Chairman.

From the University of Redlands, California, had come a representative of the University paper. The Vice-President of Paris students was there; so were four Officer Cadets from St Cyr. There were also student representatives from Burma, Scandinavia, and Holland.

Searching through reports issued by the Caux Information Service, I found that some of these young delegates had been induced to go on to the platform during Assemblies.

M. Jean-Claude Gabriel, Vice-President of the Students' Federation, Paris, was quoted as saying:

> The great family at Caux must be a pattern of a world family. . . . Next week other French students will be coming here. Together we will fight, inspired by all that Caux stands for, to achieve with students everywhere the unity which all the world needs.

And Mr Josef Römmerskirchen, Chairman of the League of Catholic Youth in Germany, had said:

> I have seen in Caux that there must be a revolution against mistrust. . . . I am convinced that the Holy Spirit is at work here at Caux. . . . With all my strength I am going to do whatever I can to bring this spirit of confidence and unity into the German youth movement.

Then the Rector of Zurich University, whose son is in the College of the Good Road, had spoken eloquently of Dr Buchman's book *Remaking the World* as " the first book in the world that shows how the ordinary man can make history."

What did all this add up to? Frankly, I didn't know. Facts were now accumulating so fast that it was impossible to sift and clarify them as I went along. It was evident, of course, that the Buchmanites were making a tremendous drive to capture the minds of young people everywhere; that they were meeting with considerable success, and were impressing older educationalists as well.

I didn't accept all that I read in that glowing prospectus for the College of the Good Road. One expects such brochures to be highly coloured, and if the Buchmanites had used every known device for embellishing their picture, such as fine printing, art paper, and profuse illustrations, that was quite legitimate. Nevertheless, I decided to re-examine that prospectus in more detail at the first opportunity.

I had heard from Mr Roger Hicks that plans were also afoot for launching a school in which younger children could be given a grounding in Buchmanite ideology before being passed on to the College of the Good Road. This, again, indicated the lengths to which these people were prepared to go in their efforts to dominate the mind of mankind.

They were modelling their methods on those of the totalitarian Powers, and admitted as much. I was told a story of someone who had visited Moscow in 1925 and who had been shown an ideological training-school where some 300 young Chinese were being prepared for Communism.

" You may not think much of this now," he was told, " but come back in twenty years' and you will find these men and women are holding the reins of their nation."

From the way the Buchmanites were setting to work it looked as if they meant to get somewhere in much less than twenty years.

I was not blind to the fact that their avowed goal was a stable world peace. How could I be when a dozen times a day one or other of their number held up Caux to me as a " microcosm of what life could be under Moral

Re-Armament "? But I was uneasy. They might be gathering the youth of all nations into their net merely to inculcate high moral principles, but it smacked too much of regimentation for my liking.

It made me more determined than ever to get behind the scenes.

CHAPTER 6

A Sinner's Sunday

DR BUCHMAN has defined " sin " as anything which keeps people from one another. And on a certain Sunday morning at Caux I must have been full of this particular brand, for I awoke with a longing to escape from Mountain House. Like Garbo, I wanted to be alone.

It was not that I was feeling unsociable. The desire was engendered by sheer necessity. Facts were piling up and so many conflicting impressions were buzzing through my brain that I couldn't see how I could sort them out unless I found some way of snatching a few moments for reflection.

I realize now that the Buchmanites don't give their visitors any time in which to think. No stranger in Mountain House is ever left to his own devices. Some full-time worker for MRA is always at his elbow to maintain a non-stop commentary on the principles of Buchmanism. This could be mere politeness—a gesture of hospitality towards a guest—but I found it much too studied to be pleasing.

I had a variety of " guides " to show me round, and every one was adept at pouring forth verbal propaganda in a ceaseless stream. They had all Dr Buchman's pet slogans by heart. It wasn't long before I was able to recite them with equal glibness. " If everybody cared enough, and everybody shared enough, wouldn't everybody have enough? " was one. " There's enough in the world for everyone's need, but not for everyone's greed " was another.

Growing accustomed to this sort of thing, I sometimes

Dr Buchman chatting with members of the cast of The Good Road.

found myself anticipating what the man at my elbow was about to say. Often I could have completed his quotations for him, but I refrained. " Everybody wants to see the other fellow changed," they would say earnestly, as if the thought had just occurred to them, though, in fact, it is one of the most popular passages in Buchmanite sloganese. " Every nation wants to see the other nation changed," it goes on. " But everybody is waiting for the other to begin."

Oddly enough, though all these sayings, and scores of others of the same kind, originated in Buchman's speeches, I never heard him use any of them himself or utter anything in the nature of a slogan.

In the course of my stay at Mountain House I was constantly re-introduced to the Master. Various " guides " in whose company I found myself on different occasions took it upon themselves to rush me forward whenever Dr Buchman chanced to be anywhere near. I lost count of the number of handshakes we exchanged. Indeed, these " introductions " grew so frequent that they became almost a joke between Dr Buchman and myself.

" Oh, I know Williamson," he would say in jocular fashion, his eyes twinkling benevolently behind his rimless spectacles. And once he inclined his head towards my ear and whispered : " We *love* ——'s," naming the proprietors of the magazine I was representing.

I was half tempted at times to abandon my inquiry and to go all out for a personal " interview " with Buchman instead. It would have been simple to have taken advantage of those multiple encounters to fire prepared queries at him, but I forebore. After all, I reflected, a full-scale interview could be obtained at any time for the asking, for Dr Buchman is always approachable. So I decided to press on with my independent probe.

In spite of all I had been shown to date, I was still far

G

from convinced that MRA was all it pretended to be.
I disliked the ceaseless barrage of flattery which poured
from the lips of most of the Buchmanites with about the
same glibness as their sloganese.

Everyone and everything was always given an enthusiastic " build up." I became accustomed to being
introduced in grandiose terms. " This is Mr Geoffrey
Williamson—a writer from London whose words go out
to many millions of people," was one flowery introduction,
but this was eclipsed by a Finnish Buchmanite who greeted
me with : " I hear you are a king among journalists."

These high-flights of imagination were embarrassing at
first, but I grew used to them and began to wonder how
I should hear myself described next. The lowest rank
ascribed to me was " Leading Features Editor for a very
powerful group." Never once was I presented as a modest
observer seeking facts. So much, I thought, for the
Buchmanite's code of " Absolute Honesty." I could
overlook this, but most of the " guides " had a manner
that was much too hearty. They were like a brisk games
mistress greeting her girls as they came off the hockey
field. In a phrase of O. Henry's, they were " too anxious
to please, to please."

*   *   *

So I wanted an armistice. Some respite, however brief,
from the " hearty " atmosphere of Mountain House. A
picture without light or shade soon palls, and I was
beginning to find that to be constantly among smiling,
affable, serene people can become just as wearisome.
I would have given anything, I felt, to see someone scowl
for a change.

Thoughts of playing truant from Caux hovered in my
mind that Sunday morning, but duty had to come first.
An Assembly of some importance was to be held, I was

told, and Lean had arranged a special luncheon party afterwards at which I was to meet a number of Far Eastern delegates. In these circumstances it was idle to dream of escape; but before I went into the Assembly I gazed longingly up the mountain-side. How pleasant it would be, I reflected, to leap upon a train bound for Rochers de Naye and leave this microcosm of a perfect world behind!

I found the Assembly differed very little from others I had attended save, as a concession to the Sabbath, the choir included a Negro spiritual and the Hallelujah Chorus in their repertoire. The speeches were variations of the same theme, expressing the hope that Moral Re-Armament would bring about better understanding between nations. Most of the speakers, too, seemed to have fallen into the habit of using Buchmanite parrot-phrases like " In order to change I must begin with myself," " change, unite, fight," " we are living in an ideological age," " inspired Democracy," " the full dimension of change," " a superior ideology," " mighty ideological weapon," and so on.

I suppose one of the brightest speeches that morning came from Senator Eleanor Butler, Acting Assistant Secretary of the Irish Labour Party. She got a laugh straight away when, explaining her reasons for visiting Caux, she said: " I thought it was a wonderful opportunity to tell a very large gathering, a much more international gathering than I could find anywhere else, some of the grievances of my country." Of course, she went on to say that she had experienced a change of heart. The big idea of Caux had made her forget her grievances.

The Senator had just come from the Strasbourg Conference, and she drew a comparison between the proceedings there and those at Caux. At Strasbourg they had lacked " what we know at Caux as a common ideology."

Towards the close of the meeting a brief, breezy speech was given by a tall, distinguished-looking man with greying hair and moustache, who was introduced as Mr Bernard M. Hallward, President, St Raymond Paper Ltd, Montreal, Canada. The name sounded familiar; groping to recall where I had heard it last, I am afraid I missed much of what the speaker had to say. But at last I remembered. He was one of the Governors of the College of the Good Road.

That interested me, but my interest was heightened further when he wound up his address with a request for funds to help carry on the good work of Moral Re-Armament. I had been assured in London that the Buchmanites never made any public appeal for funds. Yet here was Bernard Hallward, one of the movement's leading lights, not only asking us for money, but asking in a big way.

"We need three million francs!" he declared, "and we need them urgently."

He went on to explain that the money, which he was sure would be forthcoming, would be allocated equally between three main enterprises. One million would go towards the maintenance of Mountain House; one million towards the development of the College of the Good Road, and one million would be used to complete the production of *The Good Road* film.

So, while a pianist played solemn music, ushers moved silently among the audience with silver salvers which were soon heaped high with contributions. No loopholes were allowed. Those without Swiss currency or who had left their cheque books behind were given prepared slips bearing addresses in America, Australia, Britain, Ireland, and New Zealand to which financial contributions could be sent on their return home. The fact that these slips had been run off on a duplicator seemed to suggest that this practice was a fairly regular one.

I felt that it was as well that I had not played truant from that morning's Assembly. My presence had at least exploded the myth that the Buchmanites never appeal for funds.

* * *

Included in the party of Far Eastern delegates was my tea-time companion of the day before—the Lord Bishop of Rangoon. He greeted me very warmly and inquired where I proposed to sit. I said I hoped I should be placed next to him, as I should be glad of his moral support. He smiled and said that I could depend upon that.

Before luncheon I was introduced to a number of delegates, among them U Tun Nyoe, Chief Editor of *The Burma Tribune*, Rangoon, and his journalist wife, Daw Ma Ma Khin. They had brought messages from U Tin, the Burmese Minister of Finance, and from Mrs Aung San, wife of the late Burmese Premier. Both were deeply interested in Moral Re-Armament and in all that was going on at Caux. I remembered having seen them at Press conferences at Mountain House, where I had noticed that they followed proceedings with the closest interest.

I was not placed next to the Bishop, after all, but between Daw Nyein Tha, Burmese National Women's leader, and Garth Lean. As we prepared to take our seats, though, the Bishop whispered : " You'll be perfectly all right with Daw Nyein Tha next to you. You couldn't have anyone better for your purpose."

And so it proved, for Daw Nyein Tha, who was once described by the late Foreign Minister, U Tin Tut, as " the most widely known Burmese woman outside Burma," was only too ready to talk about Moral Re-Armament in that country. At twenty-one she had been headmistress of a girls' school in Burma, but I gathered that she had been an ardent supporter of Buchmanism for a number of years and had travelled through America and Europe with various task forces. She had travelled through the Ruhr with *The Good Road* show, besides appearing on platforms as an MRA speaker.

I had seen a page of pictures illustrating some of her platform "tricks" in one of the copies of *New World News* which had been given to me with other propaganda. One trick was to hold up a piece of paper, gripped firmly in each hand, and say: "When I want my way and you want your way, we pull against each other and there is tension between us."

With this she would tug the paper taut, adding: "As we pull harder, before we know it, there is a break." The paper would snap dramatically and, separating her hands, she would declaim: "If we persist in our own way, we grow farther apart!" Then, discarding the paper, she would place her hands together, as if in prayer, and say: "But when we both get back to God and want only what is right—then we are united."

A woman of most serene personality, Daw Nyein Tha talked and laughed her way through that luncheon, volunteering a wealth of information concerning her travels in general and the effect of MRA in her own country in particular. Her English was fluent, musical, and tinged, perhaps, with a slight American accent. She declared that Moral Re-Armament had spread through parts of Burma at an incredible speed.

"It was sheer force of example," she confided. "Once one village got it, other villages would want it, too, even before they understood what it was."

"Really?" I said.

"Yes," she assured me with a following peal of laughter and vigorous nodding of the head. "It spread—just like that!" She gave an eloquent flick of her hand and resumed: "You see, people in one village would note the change in another village that had got MRA. They would see that there was less drunkenness among the men of that village; less squabbling among the women. And they would see that everyone was much happier and working better. Because they worked harder and didn't waste their time drinking and fighting and idling, they became more prosperous. So, of course, that made the people in the neighbouring villages jealous, and they would say: 'We want " that thing " that the other village has got.' "

It was easy to appreciate why Daw Nyein Tha was so popular with the Buchmanites. She bubbled over with good spirits, and her heart was obviously in her work. She held my attention so closely that I hardly exchanged a word with Lean, but towards the close of the luncheon he turned to me and asked:

" What do you think you would like to do this afternoon? Is there anything you want to see especially, or would you care to rest, or what? "

I asked him what his own plans were.

" I think I shall lie down and rest for an hour or two," he said. " The next Assembly won't be till after tea."

Seeing the door of escape swing ajar, I decided that here was the chance for which I had been waiting. " Then I think I'll try to get some of my notes sorted out," I said casually. " And I might go for a stroll, or perhaps take a train up to Rochers de Naye. I've never been up there."

Leaving the " little dining-room," I ran into James Coulter, and it struck me that he would be a pleasant companion for my proposed trip up the mountain-side. He had made a good impression on me in the few encounters I had had with him. A comparative newcomer to the ranks of Moral Re-Armament, he seemed less steeped in Buchmanite lore; less prone to talk in cant phrases. It would be easier to get him on to normal topics—his wartime flying experiences, say, or his home life in Australia, where I understood his father owned a big cinema circuit.

" Got anything on this afternoon? " I queried. " I'm thinking of running up to Rochers. Care to come along? "

He received my invitation with genuine enthusiasm.

" That sounds a great idea! " he exclaimed. " I'd love to come. Thank you very much. I'll just have to hand in something at the office here, so if you care to go up to the entrance hall I'll join you there. Perhaps you wouldn't mind looking up a train? You'll see a time-table hanging in the reception office. But I shan't keep you waiting. I'll only be a couple of minutes."

I was glad I'd thought of asking him, and that the idea appealed to him. It sent me tripping up the winding stairway, elated at the prospect of getting away from Mountain House for a spell. Half-way up the stairs I came upon Dr Morris Martin and his wife engaged in some kind of light-hearted dispute.

" My wife's being very difficult," explained the doctor with a grin. " Is your wife ever difficult, Mr Williamson? "

" All wives are difficult," I answered.

" Really! " exclaimed Mrs Martin, pretending to be shocked.

" Well, what can we do about it? " demanded her husband with mock gravity. " What *can* one do when wives are difficult? "

" Nothing much," I replied. " But ' Sorry is a Magic Little Word '! "

Dr Martin looked a little taken aback, but his wife appeared delighted.

" Good for you, Mr Williamson! " she cried gleefully.

I left them both laughing together. Whatever the nature of their dispute, it appeared that I had broken the tension. And this bantering exchange told me that perhaps Buchmanites were human, after all.

* * *

There was a train leaving for Rochers de Naye in about fifteen minutes, I found, so I waited expectantly in the entrance hall, watching the doorway through which I expected Coulter to follow me. But his "couple of minutes" grew into eight, then ten, then twelve, without his putting in an appearance.

I wondered if there could have been any misunderstanding, and whether he had meant the entrance to the station. It was barely a hundred yards away, so I hurried along to the platform. A train came up from Glion and departed on the steep ascent to Rochers de Naye, but there was no sign of Coulter. And, glancing at the time indicator, I saw that there would not be another train for half an hour or so.

Chafing at the delay, I strolled back to the vestibule of Mountain House and resumed my vigil there. What could have delayed Coulter like this, I wondered? I wandered along the *promenoir* and took a swift look round the Press Room; but he was not there. So I went back to the entrance hall, deciding that I would give him five minutes more; and if he hadn't turned up then I would go without him. I didn't want to miss another train.

I was, in fact, on the point of leaving when Lean came bustling towards me. "Coulter's got a special job to do," he announced breathlessly. "I'm coming with you instead."

Lean assured me that he didn't mind missing his siesta. He would much rather join me on my jaunt to Rochers—if I didn't object.

I didn't object, of course, but Coulter had displayed

such eagerness to come with me, that I was sorry he couldn't join us.

It seemed very sporting of Lean to sacrifice his Sunday afternoon nap in order to save me from a lonely excursion.

I felt that it would be a useful opportunity for a discussion with Lean away from the artificial atmosphere of Mountain House. It might easily enable me to clear up a few points. Not that I was much in the mood for intensive cross-questioning or for bothering my head very much about problems of Buchmanism that afternoon. I wanted to relax and enjoy the scenery.

Wonderful vistas engaged the eye wherever one chose to look. Impressive glimpses of passes and valleys and slopes unfolded as the train climbed steadily upwards. Far below, the Lake of Geneva stretched into infinity, with the roofs of Territet and Montreux and Vevey shimmering in the sunshine. Already I felt a subtle suggestion of freedom. When Lean pointed out the picturesque slopes of Caux below us, with Mountain House being fast reduced to the proportions of a tiny chalet, I knew that I was getting things into true perspective.

Stepping from the train into a silent world of grey peaks at Rochers—" the Rigi of the Western Alps "—was to experience even greater exhilaration. We made for the observation platform, a few hundred feet above the station, toiling up the zig-zag path at leisurely pace, with frequent pauses for breath. At 6,700 feet—twice the height of Caux—the rarefied air needed getting used to.

When we finally gained the observation platform we rested for some time, talking little, but enjoying the impressive panorama, which embraces all the summits of the Bernese Oberland and part of the chains of Mont Blanc and Valais. Looking down across the vast valleys, we saw the entire fifty-mile expanse of the Lake of Geneva stretched out in a delicate haze.

But it was the endless panorama of the peaks which most fascinated me, though I thought they lacked the sublime grandeur of Schynige Platte, in the Oberland, which I had visited two years before. There the splendour had been overwhelming in its compactness; here it was spread more widely and lost something by diffusion.

Later, strolling back towards the railway station, we paused at a point from which Mountain House was visible again. It didn't seem to matter at all now, but my companion asked tentatively whether I had yet been able to form any conclusions about the Group and its work.

I told him that I had been interested in all I had been shown, which was true; and I added that I thought it surprising that the world's Press had more or less ignored the Assembly at Caux.

" The English papers, perhaps," he said hastily. " But not the European. We get a very good Press in most European countries, where they are closer to realities and understand ideological warfare much better than those who have no frontier problems. But what do you yourself think of Caux? "

" I've yet to make up my mind," I replied. " But, of course, I appreciate the Group's general aim of trying to foster international understanding." I went on to say that I thought most people would recognize that the mere act of drawing representatives of so many different nations to the World Assembly was in itself a considerable achievement, whatever ideologies one favoured.

As for the doctrines, they were, I supposed, likely to appeal to people of goodwill everywhere, whatever their religion or background. Most thinking people knew in their hearts that there would always be strife in the world until nations learned to curb rivalries and jealousies and devised some formula for living together in harmony.

The idea of educating people for peace instead of war was one which many thinkers had entertained. And most people worked through, as a matter of experience, to a realization that moral order must precede political order.

"That's true enough," agreed Lean. "I grant you a lot of people *think* these things; but very few *do* anything about it. Dr Buchman has taken the basic truths which you and I learnt at our mothers' knee and made them effective in the lives of thousands of people."

"I appreciate that," I told him. "But I've collected too many impressions to be able to digest them all at once. I'm afraid the evaluation I attempted just now was a little sketchy."

"But I think it was a very fair evaluation," was his reply, and we left it at that.

Though not very profound, this discussion amid the rugged Alpine peaks was our most serious exchange since my arrival in Switzerland. No doubt it was engendered by the intoxicating mountain air, yet I was perfectly sincere in acknowledging the value of some of Dr Buchman's teachings. After all, there was nothing new in his ideas. Stripped of cant phrases and an artificial aura of mysticism, those ideas were nothing but a paraphrase of the Ten Commandments and the Sermon on the Mount.

Be honest; unselfish; chaste—and love thy neighbour as thyself. That was the core of the matter; yet around that core the Buchmanites had spun a cocoon of fantasy. The basic truths still shone through, just as the waters of that vast lake spread out below us gleamed through the gathering haze. But something remained hidden; something which I had yet to discover.

The warehouse of my mind was becoming congested with merchandise that was bewildering in its variety. Hard facts mingled with illusions generated by the

Buchmanites' efficient propaganda machine: they would have to be separated somehow. My transitory impressions would have to give way to considered judgment. Meanwhile my fact gathering had to continue.

We had tea on the roof of the hotel above the railway station, and caught the next train down to Caux. Lean said, with evident satisfaction, that it would get us back before the afternoon Assembly ended. As it happened, the proceedings were very nearly over when we finally got back to Mountain House, but I didn't mind that. I had had my brief release and felt appreciably refreshed, but I was still not in the mood to enjoy an Assembly.

In fairness, I must record that others were not of the same mind. The hall was packed. Every seat was taken, and people were standing three and four deep in the side aisles and at the back. I squeezed in on the fringe of this great throng in time to hear U Ba Lwin, a Burmese educationalist, read a message from the Prime Minister of Burma, Thakin Nu:

> A re-assessment of our moral values and their application to our problems [the message ran] is a vital necessity today. Discussions which contribute towards such a re-assessment will have a beneficial effect on world problems.
>
> The first objective of the people of the world should be to acquire the right conception of life. Although within easy reach of this they still fail to grasp it because of their indifference. This failure is the main cause of the present world disorder.
>
> The answer will be the same, no matter whether it is for westerner or easterner, exploiter or exploited, Christian or non-Christian. It lies in the right conception of life.
>
> To those who have achieved this conception, materialistic objectives which can give only fleeting satisfaction, shorter in duration than the twinkling of an eye, will no longer constitute the main objective. The good road to eternal bliss will with them become the main goal, and this alone can give permanent satisfaction.
>
> The day when this main objective reassumes its proper place will be the day when real peace will appear in the world.
>
> So long as the people of the world do not achieve this realization, neither atomic energy nor ideal resolutions nor endless sermons will bring real peace and unity to humanity.

This message, impressively read, sentence by sentence, to enable a German interpreter to follow up with a free translation, as usual, brought the entire gathering to its feet. The applause was terrific, and deservedly so, I think, for the sender had articulated the main arguments for Moral Re-Armament with greater clarity than was evinced in many of the Buchmanite pamphlets I had read.

That particular Assembly was devoted almost wholly to the Orient. An American professor who had just flown back from China gave some account of his travels, and moved the audience visibly when he told of encounters with people who remembered Dr Buchman's visits of more than thirty years ago.

There was one " fine old character," he declared, known as " Mother Wu," who had asked him to bring a gift for " Frank," as Dr Buchman is almost universally called by his followers. The presentation was made on the spot— a box of handkerchiefs embroidered by Mother Wu herself.

Later came another presentation, made by U Tun Nyoe, of Rangoon, Chief Editor of *The Burma Tribune*. This was a bronze statuette of a " Phongyi "—Buddhist monk— depicted in rapt contemplation of the Buddhist scriptures written upon palm leaves. It was said to be the work of one of Burma's master smiths, U Ohn, of Rangoon.

Great excitement attended both presentations, but though the applause was prolonged, Dr Buchman could not be prevailed upon to make a speech. After one great outburst it looked as if he was wavering, for he held up a hand to restore silence. The clapping and the cheering died away, and in the expectant hush which followed, the Master's voice was heard.

" Close the windows! " he commanded imperiously. " Too much air! "

Then he sat down. Nobody laughed. Nobody but me, that is. And my mirth was due to a remembrance of another occasion on which he had played the same card. Only then his command had been: "Open the windows!"

*　　*　　*

That same evening Dr Buchman sent forth an edict of a different kind. I was invited to dine at his table, an honour usually reserved for his most distinguished guests. I was at a loss to know why I was being so favoured. Could it possibly be that Lean had passed on the gist of our conversation on the mountain-top that afternoon? Had my innocent remark about appreciating the Group's general aim of trying to foster international understanding been interpreted as indicating sympathies? Had my companion leapt to the conclusion that I was " as good as changed "? And was this high honour of a seat at the Master's table the next move in an attempt to draw me deeper into the fold?

Whatever the answer, it would be a pleasant wind-up to my " Sinner's Sunday."

I found myself placed between an American couple, the man being none other than the professor who had just flown in from China and who I had heard speaking on the platform barely an hour before. His wife had come to Caux to meet him, leaving their children in the States.

They were charming to talk to and very natural. Within a minute family snapshots were being brought out for my inspection. You would have thought that this couple, who had been separated for a long time, would have resented having a " foreign " Pressman planted between them when they must have had so much they wanted to say to each other; but, no. They were gracious and friendly. We all got along well.

Across the table I spied another friendly face. James Coulter had also been honoured. He caught my eye and shot me a knowing smile. I guessed that this was a

" treat " for him as compensation for having missed his jaunt to Rochers de Naye that afternoon.

That dinner was a memorable one—a real Southern feast, doubtless in tribute to my American companions. There were lots of flowers on the table, which was beautifully set with sparkling cutlery; and we had fine damask napkins—not paper ones, as at the other tables. And the food was superb.

There was sweet-corn soup, rich in cream—a truly ambrosial liquid. I have tasted no soup to equal it, before or since. Then came genuine Virginian ham, with delicious *sauté* potatoes, garnished with just a shred of onion. And, cooked with the ham, was a peeled peach, studded with cloves. Salad was also served.

How do I know that it was genuine ham from Lil' Ole Virginny? The American professor's wife assured me that it was. I always like to get my facts corroborated by an expert when I can.

And then the sweet! How can I convey in words the masterpiece that was set before me? There is pie and pie. This was the pie to end all pies. Pecan-nut pie to be precise. A factual description would be—a segment of pastry, a layer of treacle, a layer of pecan nuts and a layer of meringue. But surely there could be nothing factual about the pie I ate that night. It was a poem of perfection.

My American friends were pleased to hear me rhapsodize.

" Frank has always taught our girls to take great pains with their cooking," the professor's wife explained to me. " He says that that is one of the ways in which they can express the love they feel for their families."

I thought if this was a sample of the kind of meals which found their way to Buchman's table, the hearts of those slaving away in the kitchens must be loving indeed.

" Do you enjoy cooking? " I asked my companion.

She sat suddenly upright.

" Gee! " she cried. " I couldn't cook a meal like this to save my life! But I wouldn't tell my family that! "

Such a wonderful meal merited undivided concentration, yet between soup and coffee I contrived to absorb some information from my newly-made American friends. The professor assured me that he had not exaggerated in saying from the platform that Dr Buchman was still remembered by people he had met in China as far back as 1918. He had met many, besides " Mother Wu," so it was evident that Dr Buchman must have made a very great impression. They not only remembered him; they revered him.

From his wife I gained a little information about the Buchmanite training centre on Mackinac Island. " I'd say it was a small-scale Caux," she declared. " Yes; that about fits it, I guess. Say, have you noticed something? I keep wanting to put all my talk in one-syllable words! You see, I met so many of the Eastern delegates this afternoon, that I can't get out of the way of making everything I say simple. You know the sort of thing— ' Me want tell you this. . . .' and so on. Excuse me."

She confided that there had been a little trouble at Mackinac. People had tried hard to get the Buchmanites out. She suspected the local vice ring of being at the bottom of it all. There were liquor racketeers and others who resented the coming of MRA, apparently. They had regarded the island as their exclusive territory, and they feared for their livelihood.

*   *   *

After that epic repast Lean announced that he had arranged for me to see another performance of *The Good Road*—if I was agreeable. In my replete condition I think

H

I would have agreed to anything; but what really swayed me was the intimation that James Coulter would accompany me. I took this to be another sop to Coulter to make up for that missed trip.

The man was certainly eager to see the show, although he said he had lost count of the number of performances he had attended. He was in high spirits. He had been given two excellent seats in about the fifth row.

Before the curtain rose he asked me how I had enjoyed the dinner, and he grinned broadly when I extolled its merits. He said that as soon as he had been told that he was to dine at Buchman's table he had sneaked into the kitchens to try to find what the menu was to be. " Never you mind," they had told him, " but you'll get a meal tonight that you'll never forget ! " Their prophecy was pretty sound.

It was a gala night in the theatre. The Mayor of Montreux was there with his family, a row or two ahead of us. And out in front, between stage and audience, Dr Buchman had his characteristic sideways perch, left shoulder to the stage, right towards the auditorium.

Now, whether some of the champagne air of Rochers de Naye was still lingering in the system, or whether it was the influence of that ambrosial feast, I viewed this second performance with an almost benign tolerance. Crudities that had jarred on the previous night now slipped past. And the players were putting such tremendous gusto into their performance, and obviously enjoying themselves so intensely, that I felt they deserved all the applause they got.

I still thought the propaganda was dragged in too brazenly and that a little subtlety would have rendered many of the scenes far more effective. And there was a *non sequitur* about the whole thing. But it did have points. The music was better than I had thought. There were several quite catchy tunes. After the show, light refreshments were served in an ante-room, the hard-working players themselves coming straight from the stage to wait upon the guests. One of the attractive daughters of U Tin Tut, first Foreign Minister of Burma, brought me cocoa and biscuits.

" It's a shame to make you do this, when you've been working so hard on the stage," I said.

" We enjoy it," she answered with a smile.

And, looking round at the other happy players, it was obvious that they did.

Coulter, being quartered down in Glion, had to leave me, but Dr William Reed, the show's musical director, slipped into his vacant seat to ask me what I had thought of the show. I told him that I thought it well staged, but that some of its better features would be lost in the film. For example, all the vivid colourings of the international costumes in the opening scenes and in the finale would be missed.

He agreed, but thought that might be compensated for in some measure by the greater scope offered by the camera for close-ups and for portraying movement.

I said that catchy tune, *Come Along, It's an Invitation*, was buzzing through my brain. He agreed that it was " a delightful thing." The composer was Shelagh Stevenson. All the songs from *The Good Road* had been recorded by a famous gramophone company. We chatted for a long time, and when I finally talked of retiring, Dr Reed insisted on setting me on my way.

I found Lean already in bed. And when he asked if I had enjoyed my day, I could truthfully say that I had. I felt so benign at that moment that I would have signed blank cheques for any Buchmanites who had asked for them! But that spell was not to last. In the morning something was to happen to break it completely.

CHAPTER 7

Tears in the Morning

ALONE in my room for a moment, making a quick check-up on my notes, for it was my last morning at Caux, I was distracted suddenly by the sounds of convulsive sobbing somewhere outside my window. It happened without any audible prelude that I was aware of. Comparative silence had reigned a second before; then had come this sudden flood of grief. Crossing the room, I saw vaguely through the french windows the slim figure of a girl in a white blouse darting across the lawn towards the far end of the terrace. Her distress was all too apparent, for she sobbed aloud as she ran. And though she was out of view in a few seconds, the sound of her sobs still reached me.

Hastily I gathered my papers together and stuffed them into my attaché case, for the incident had stirred my curiosity.

You may say that an unknown girl's grief was no concern of mine; but I scented a story. In any other place or in any other circumstances it might have seemed of no great moment. But for such a thing to occur at Caux, where all was serenity, and smiling faces were the rule, was unthinkable. Why, among the thousands of visitors, should this one girl be unhappy? I meant to find out.

So, darting through the french windows, I followed the pathway to the lawn and hurried in the direction taken by the running girl. But though quite a few people were strolling upon the terrace or standing about in groups, chatting, I was unable to identify anyone as approximating to the figure I had seen. Feeling just a little foolish, though still decidedly curious, I strolled back to my room.

*   *   *

Rival attractions were presented for my consideration that morning. I was given the choice of attending an early morning class of the College of the Good Road, or a lecture in the theatre on " The Significance of the Life and Work of Frank Buchman." Without intending any slight on the students, I chose the latter. I felt I had already gathered sufficient information about the College, and the prospect of learning something about the founder and leader of the Oxford Group was, frankly, more alluring.

Lean heartily endorsed my choice. The Good Road pupils, it appeared, would simply be studying the newspapers during that particular session. " Just to gain some general knowledge of world events," Lean explained. " There really wouldn't be much in it for you."

The lecture on Dr Buchman was delivered by Alan Thornhill, whose name was growing quite familiar to me by this time, for he seemed to have a finger in every Buchmanite pie. Besides being the author of *The Forgotten Factor* and part author of *The Good Road* revue, he was, you may remember, one of the Governors of the College of the Good Road.

That he was proving an attraction was evident from the size of the audience which had gathered in the theatre. Thornhill opened his talk by expressing his appreciation of the fact that so many people had come to a lecture at 7 a.m. on a Monday morning. Anyone will realize that it can't be easy to enthuse a sleepy audience which has not had its breakfast, but Thornhill, being obviously fired by his theme, struggled valiantly to do so.

I followed his address carefully because I knew he had

been closely associated with Buchman for many years. In the main it was an interesting talk, though much of it was familiar to me, as I had recently read an appraisement of Buchman which Thornhill had contributed to *Remaking the World*.

He presented Buchman as something of a split personality, I thought, though perhaps not intentionally. On the one hand he recounted various pleasing anecdotes designed to show his chief as a very human character, a great " mixer," and ever preoccupied with people. On the other hand, he tried to present Buchman as a gifted visionary, heaven-sent.

Thus, at one moment he was telling us how " Frank " had once taken twelve girls to a dance " rather than leave anyone out." And the next he was emphasizing " Frank's " high spiritual qualities. Or again, he told how the cook in the Buchman home in Pennsylvania always used to say that she never knew how many places to lay for dinner because one could never tell whom Frank would meet on the way home. And this was followed by a dissertation upon Destiny. " It was no accident," he declared, " that Frank Buchman was born into this century—and no accident that he was born an American."

Inevitably the lecture was peppered with Buchmanite jargon and a few of Frank's pronouncements, such as: " The Oxford Group is a big lake where a lamb can wade and an elephant can swim," or " It's no good throwing eye-medicine out of a second-storey window."

Introduced into the body of this lecture was an " explanation " of why some people were privileged to take their meals in the " little dining-room," which struck me as odd, to say the least. " Some people may require a different kind of food," said the lecturer. " It may be that they have reached a higher stage of spiritual development."

This was the first mention of spiritual development that I had heard during my stay at Mountain House, though I had privately noted that some of Dr Buchman's followers, especially those closest to him, did at times present what may well be described as a " spiritual look." They betrayed a certain brightness of eye, offset by a darkness round the sockets, an ashen complexion, and a marked transparency of skin. This I thought to be most noticeable as they emerged from their early morning " Quiet Time." It seemed to betoken the great emotional stress to which they had subjected themselves.

Although I was not yet in a position to make a full assessment of all I had noted at Mountain House, certain facts kept thrusting themselves into the forefront of my thoughts. The whole system of Buchmanism seemed riddled with incongruities.

First, there was a suggestion of snobbishness about their policies which hardly measured up to the repeated talk about " inspired democracy." I have already mentioned the way in which everyone was given a superlative " build-up " whenever introductions were being effected, usually exaggerating their attainments, as in my own case, or laying particular emphasis upon titles or good family connections. " He's the son of so-and-so," or " His cousin is the Duke of so-and-so."

It was also manifest that it was the Buchmanites' unswerving policy to cultivate the wealthy and the influential and to display less concern for the underdog. A small nucleus of ordinary folk, miners, steelworkers, shipyard hands, and others was included, to be sure, and some of these were put forward on the platform at every opportunity. But I noted that the individuals selected in this respect were usually men in key positions in their industry—shop stewards, union officials or people who might be expected to influence their fellow workers.

My perusal of some of the Buchmanite literature had shown me, too, that a handful of these " types " kept cropping up with amazing frequency in one enterprise after another. Some had figured in campaigns in a number of countries, which seemed to argue that they were a regular part of a Buchman " Circus."

Another point which stood out clearly was that all the full-time officials seemed to reflect an affluence which hardly seemed compatible with the fact that they were all said to be working without salary. Most of them had clothes of Savile Row quality and cut. A lot of them had smart cars at their disposal.

It was also self-evident that money was being expended with prodigal extravagance in nearly every field. The catering at Caux was of a quality to match that in the best luxury hotels. And the whole atmosphere (with the exception of a temporary lack of boiler fuel) was one of ostentatious prosperity. I had noticed much the same sort of thing in London. So I couldn't help reflecting that even if the organization could count upon a generous flow of gifts in cash and kind, and save expense by relying upon volunteer labour, its way of life was extravagant in the extreme.

Against all this I had evidence that scores of highly intelligent men, scholars, statesmen, and men of action, warmly supported the Group. Yet if I had noticed the inconsistencies they must have noticed them, too. I had plenty of riddles to take back with me to London.

*   *   *

From the lecture I went to breakfast, joining a small party of Norwegian students. They were enthralled by all they saw at Caux. It was wonderful to meet so many people from so many countries. Such a gathering must surely have a great influence in cementing understanding and fostering world peace. They hoped to come again.

I took a stroll upon the terrace again, scanning the faces of the polyglot crowds. Yes, it did seem a wonderful gathering. There were many girls with white blouses among the throng, but all looked radiantly happy. It was hard to imagine that any of them had ever shed a tear. Yet, somewhere in that vast assembly, I knew, must be the girl whose bitter weeping I had heard not so long before. The mystery tantalized me. It was stupid that the incident should linger in my mind when I had so many other problems with which to wrestle.

One of these was purely domestic. I was wondering how I could steal away and slip down into Montreux to do some shopping. I wanted a few souvenirs for the folks at home. When I consulted the time-table I found that the trains were hopeless; so I sought out Lean and, explaining my desire, asked if I could be fixed up with a car. His face fell and he looked genuinely pained to think that I was ready to play truant from Mountain House on my last morning. But he promised to help.

" Of course," he said. " We'll fix you up. Someone is sure to be going down for something or other. But there's an Assembly at eleven, you know. We're trying to make it an all-British affair, and we were wondering whether you'd care to go on the platform and say something? "

I pondered a moment. His tone implied that he attached immense importance to the Assembly, but his suggestion that I should participate was startling. I recalled the song of the night before: *Come Along, it's an Invitation !* Did they really think I could be lured on to that platform? I shook my head.

" Thanks, but I think not. I really want to get a few presents for the family. It will be my only chance."

" You could attend the Assembly, and I'd run you down afterwards. There'd still be time. Won't you change your mind? "

" About speaking? "

" Yes."

" I'd rather not. But I can get back for the Assembly all right, because my shopping won't take long."

Lean was visibly crestfallen, but he quickly found someone who was bound for Montreux on business. This proved to be another member of the Council of Management, a Mr Lawson Wood. He was taking his car to be looked at, he said, but he would not be staying very long in Montreux, as he was anxious to get back for the Assembly at eleven. I told him that would suit me, and off we went. It was a speedy run down, by way of Glion, and my companion dropped me immediately the first parade of shops was reached.

While he went on to his garage I set off on a quick quest for nylons and other items. He arranged to pick me up again in twenty-five minutes. Montreux seemed like a ghost town that morning, for the season was ended. Forlorn rows of tables and chairs stood outside the numerous cafés. Zurchers, which a month or so before had been crowded to capacity morning, noon, and night, had one solitary customer, I noticed, and he looked like a native.

Shops which I had seen packed with eager holiday-makers were now deserted ; but, pressed as I was for time, this proved a decided advantage. My few modest purchases were soon made, and I was back at the appointed spot, waiting to be picked up. The car came gliding to the kerb, on time to the minute, and we raced back to Mountain House, arriving just before the Assembly opened.

Apparently the organizers had dressed the platform

strongly for their All-British gathering—the last function of the kind I was to attend at Mountain House. One of their full-time officials, a Scot, whom I recognized as a member of *The Good Road* cast, was in the chair. He made a forceful opening speech, and introduced his mixed bag of speakers with confidence. There was a Socialist M.P., a Welsh miner, a society family, and a family of title.

Where, I wondered, should I have fitted in, had I accepted Lean's invitation to go on the platform and " say something "? I had no qualms about having refused that request. I knew my decision was the right one. After all, I was there as an observer, and to have spoken from that platform, however discreetly, would have weakened my claim of impartiality.

The Assembly was no more inspiring than any of the others I had attended. It followed the same pattern, with the choir working hard to provide appropriate atmosphere. There was the *Westminster Song* to welcome the Socialist M.P., and the *Rhondda Song* for the miner, both rendered with a great deal of fervour.

I have quite forgotten how the families were heralded. It may have been with *Sorry is a Magic Little Word* or *Families Can Be Fun*. I was not terribly interested. Nor, I imagined, were all those distinguished delegates who had travelled across the world to attend what they had been led to believe was an important international conference.

> This special Assembly will be an unrivalled opportunity to create and strengthen the ideological links between nations upon which the unity of Europe and the future of civilization depends.

Again I recalled the bait that had gone out with the invitation cards. " Critical world events face all leaders in the immediate weeks ahead. . . ." Yet here was a miner telling the Assembly how, before being " changed " by MRA, he had been in the habit of pilfering scraps of wood from the pit where he was employed; and a school-boy from Eton was adding his solemn testimony to the effect that he would rather be up at Caux than down in Montreux.

The level was raised by the Member of Parliament, a staunch supporter of Moral Re-Armament, who left the Assembly in no doubt as to his sincerity. He had seen it work in industry, he declared, and he was convinced that the fundamentals latent in it were going to solve the problems of the future.

But the meeting slumped badly with the family " confessions " which followed. Frankly, I was baffled, for I could not imagine how such fatuous proceedings could possibly contribute anything towards the solution of world problems.

A mother told with charming sincerity how MRA had made her resolve to try to understand her children better; how she had previously tended to look at their faults, and not pause to think that there might be faults on her side, too.

A demure debutante, fresh from the London " Season," told how the aimlessness of social life had shocked her; another schoolboy, two sizes larger than the first, told how he and his brother had always formed an anti-parent society before MRA changed their outlook and moved them to be more co-operative.

More testimony followed from a group of sisters, who prompted their recollections by consulting little black note-books. One by one, with the utmost gravity, they " confessed " to petty jealousies of each other's looks. " I used to be very jealous of my sisters because I thought people took more notice of them than me . . ." is a fair sample of the kind of thing to which that vast international gathering was obliged to listen that morning. I thought it an affront to busy statesmen and other distinguished guests, a waste of their valuable time and an imposition on their tolerance.

Had I been anywhere near a doorway I think I would have walked out, so indignant did I feel; but I was hemmed in the centre of a row, far from any exit. I sought solace in the thought that the meeting would soon be over, and that I should be back home that night.

And then a thunderbolt! The last speaker rose to give her testimony, a pretty girl who appeared from her manner to be somewhat nervous. She, too, clutched a little black note-book tightly in her hands. Another jealous sister! I thought, and yet . . . Her face was pale—almost as pale as the white blouse she was wearing. Her hesitancy vanished as she faced the audience and said: "When I heard this morning that we were to appear on this platform as a united family, I ran into the garden and burst into tears."

Those on the platform exchanged surprised glances. There was an embarrassing hush. The audience was shaken, though no one could have been more moved than I was by this unexpected development. The girl, colour returning to her cheeks, plunged on to say in effect that though she had carefully weighed the pros and cons of Moral Re-Armament, she was not at all sure that she was prepared to support it whole-heartedly. She doubted if she could bring herself to the point of sacrificing her individuality.

She had apparently compromised this morning and had allowed herself to be persuaded to go on the platform with the other members of her family. Her frankness was quite disarming. "If it really makes for peace and better understanding," she concluded, "then I am prepared to give MRA a trial. *But I still don't like it.*"

And so ended that Assembly.

I left the hall feeling rewarded for having sat it out.

The mystery of the weeping girl was solved. Odd that she should have been the very last speaker that morning; still more odd that she should have been the first among all the speakers I had heard during my stay at Caux with the courage to venture a dissenting voice. And it was courage: moral courage of a high order. It must have required nerve and strength of character, I reflected, to stand up in that huge gathering and to dare to cast a doubt upon the attractiveness of MRA. Yet that was what this girl had done.

Somehow or other she had been coaxed into appearing on the platform; but, thank heaven! she had preserved her individual point of view. Something told me that she always would; that the Buchmanites were not likely to find it easy to " change " a person who so obviously preferred to reason things out for herself.

*   *   *

Lean had suggested that I might like to take my farewell luncheon in the cafeteria for a change, especially as time was short. The coach was due to leave for Geneva within an hour. I readily agreed, because, except for break-fasts, I had taken all my meals so far in the " little dining-room," and I thought it would be as well to find out how the masses fared.

But the plan did not mature, for before we could reach the counter a messenger intercepted us. " Dr Buchman has given instructions that all those leaving on the special plane for London are to be given luncheon at his table," he told Lean. An edict from " Frank " was not to be disregarded, so we promptly headed for the " little dining-room."

The Master's table had been laid for us, but Buchman was not present. He was resting in his suite, Lean explained. He had had some very strenuous days lately and, at seventy-one, it was necessary for him to take things quietly now and then. But he had not forgotten that a plane-load of guests was departing that day. His thoughtful gesture in ordering a special luncheon for them, to be served at his own table, was typical of his good nature.

Of course, it was an excellent luncheon, though hardly so superlative as the dinner of the preceding night. Lean sat beside me, and I recognized some people who had flown out with me, though not all. It appeared that certain guests were making a longer stay, which accounted for the variation in the passenger list. Among those remaining was Powell, the strike leader, whom I had not seen since our encounter in the theatre. But I was to hear of him again.

Lean was remaining at Caux, too, so over luncheon we ran through a number of points to make sure that I had seen all there was to see and had gathered all the facts I desired. I said that I thought I had ample material, but that if I found myself in need of further enlightenment before his return to London I would contact Captain Dilly at Hay's Mews.

"That's right," said Lean. "And you can always have a message sent to me by teleprinter, you know. We exchange messages with Hay's Mews twice daily."

I said I would remember that, but doubted whether it would be necessary to trouble him in that way.

"Well, you'll be home tonight," went on Lean. "I expect they'll be glad to see you. And tomorrow you'll be back in your office, I suppose?"

"Yes; I shall have to get down to work."

"That's right. You'll have to apply a certain portion of your anatomy to your chair and produce your report. How long do you think that will take you?"

"I couldn't say. I've got so many notes and so much

reading matter to study that it may take some time, especially if I have to sandwich it in with other assignments, which is quite likely.''

" I see," said Lean.   " Well, let me know how it works out.''

By the time luncheon was over the coach was waiting at the entrance to Mountain House. Luggage was stowed and passengers were beginning to climb aboard when Lean announced that Dr Buchman wished to say good-bye to me. He hurried me through to the Master's suite, and I stood aside while he knocked on one door and held a whispered conversation with someone just inside. There was a very brief pause, and I was conducted along the passage to a second door and ushered into the presence.

Accustomed to seeing everything at Mountain House done on the grand scale, I had prepared myself for an impressive audience. Instead, Dr Buchman greeted me in his pyjamas, unshaven, unembarrassed, lolling back against the pillows, completely relaxed. Scattered remains of a luncheon which had not been relished, apparently, littered a tray lying askew in his lap. One nude foot protruded stiffly from beneath the disarranged bedclothes, thrust forth at a defiant angle with more consideration for personal comfort than for æstheticism.

The good man was not alone, for a little circle of young acolytes hovered attentively in the background, their smartly-tailored suits contrasting oddly with their leader's crumpled pyjamas. Why, I wondered, had Dr Buchman elected to exhibit himself to me without his cloak? Was it to demonstrate that he could dispense with ceremony and be wholly natural when he chose? Was it a gesture of contempt for all convention? Was it that he was too exhausted to care how he looked or who saw him?

He certainly presented a pathetic spectacle. A tired old man, worn out with the strain of a lifetime's battling for an ideal. Whether one accepted that ideal, or whether one thought it an illusion, it was impossible not to respect the tenacity with which he had pursued his purpose.

As I approached the bedside, avoiding the sentinel of that outstretched foot, Dr Buchman extended a hand, semi-deformed with arthritis. But he remained silent. His acolytes were silent. I was silent. The situation was so grotesquely different from anything I had conjured up in my mind's eye that I was nonplussed. I have been ushered into the presence of many famous personalities in my time, but I had never experienced a reception quite like this.

At last, to break the prolonged tension, I blurted out some words of thanks for all the hospitality I had received during my stay at Mountain House. I said that I had been well looked after and much appreciated the facilities which I had been given for making my inquiries.

" Fine! " murmured Dr Buchman with no show of interest.

Again an awful silence descended upon the room. I wanted to bolt without appearing rude.

" They're keeping the coach waiting for me," I said. " So I must say good-bye. But I'm taking back a lot of interesting impressions of Caux; some of them very deep impressions. . . ."

But even this flowery farewell failed to draw the slightest response beyond a repeated murmur of: " Fine! " Dr Buchman's face was a mask of almost Oriental inscrutability.

So I retreated in confusion under the curious gaze of the attendant bodyguard, who stood in line, mute and equally inscrutable. In a visit crowded with incongruous incidents and surprises that farewell " audience " with Buchmanism's chief and founder lingers as my queerest memory of all.

*   *   *

I

Maid Marian was waiting for us on the tarmac at Cointrin Airport, and we took off promptly, after a minimum of formality at the Customs. It was good to be speeding homeward; good to be able to relax, free for the time being from the necessity of listening, observing, and absorbing. Now I could sit back and think.

It is not surprising, perhaps, with the memory of that strange farewell so fresh in my mind, that my thoughts dwelt first upon that semi-mystical character, Dr Buchman. The very magnitude of his achievements commanded respect. Starting with nothing but an idea, he had contrived to build up a powerful organization with world-wide implications. His movement owned a mansion in Berkeley Square, and, by all the outward and visible signs, a treasure-chest with seemingly limitless resources.

Was he a charlatan? I did not think so. Peter Howard had posed precisely the same question in one of his books and had answered it with an emphatic " No! " though at that time he and Dr Buchman had never met. I had studied Dr Buchman fairly closely, but I did not find it so easy to make up my mind.

Another possibility presented itself. Buchman rarely spoke nowadays and his writings were surprisingly few. His latest book, *Remaking the World*, struck me as a " scissors-and-paste " job, merely a collection of old speeches. There had not even been enough of those to make a book. The volume was padded out with eulogies and biographical notes from half a dozen contributors. . . . Could it be, then, that Buchman was being exploited as a figure-head by some of his followers?

And who were those followers? Were they sincere men and women who had truly sacrificed all personal ambition to devote their lives to the task of spreading a gospel in which they themselves whole-heartedly believed? Were they merely sybarites who, beaten by the struggle of life, preferred to live in luxury on the bounty which Buchmanism seemed to provide?

At this stage in my inquiries I was still in doubt on these and many other points. At one moment I was ready to believe one thing; but the next moment would find me wavering. The secret of Buchmanism was as elusive as quicksilver. Just as you imagined that it was firmly in your grasp it oozed through your fingers and left you empty-handed.

How was I to bring this puzzling inquiry to a satisfactory conclusion? I wanted to be fair. I was determined to sift and weigh my evidence carefully. But some inner instinct kept telling me that Buchmanism was not wholly what it seemed. I simply could not accept it at its face value.

A clean-shaven stranger in a seat just across the aisle broke in upon my thoughts with some remark or other. Presently we were in conversation and he was asking me what I thought of Caux and whether it was my first visit. After we had compared notes in a non-committal sort of way I let him know that my mission to Caux had been purely that of an independent observer. He asked me if I had seen *The Good Road*. I said I had seen it twice and had viewed some of the film " rushes," too.

" Then you *have* been privileged! " he declared. " My wife and I haven't seen those—and our daughter is in the film; she plays the English girl."

Immediately I knew who the stranger was. He was Mr. John Nowell, manager of one of the largest sole-leather tanneries in the North of England.

He seemed surprised that I knew his name and remembered his daughter, Christine Nowell. I told him I had seen her on the set at Lausanne when visiting the studio in July.

"You must have a remarkable memory," he said.

I let it go at that. It would have been too troublesome to explain that I had read quite a lot about his daughter in various Buchmanite publications—and quite a lot about him, too. He was evidently a staunch supporter of Moral Re-Armament.

In one article in *New World News* I had read about his application of MRA methods in his tannery. He was quoted as saying:

> I have proved again and again the truth that honest apology is the mightiest weapon that anyone can wield. It is the foundation stone of that confidence on which alone can be built the new democracy that industry must find. Teamwork spreading from home to industry must be the pattern for a world that works.

He said much the same to me on the plane, though in colloquial language. But he said he had not influenced his daughter in any way. The decision to devote her life to the cause of Moral Re-Armament had been her own. He was glad that she had taken it. So, without seeking it, I had gathered more testimony to add to my already formidable amount of data. Here was a hard-headed business-man, obviously sincere, obviously shrewd and thoughtful, telling me frankly that he believed in Buchmanism. . . . I could see that a lot more probing lay ahead of me.

We made good progress, flying high at 8,500 feet. The sun went down, sinking like a luminous orange into billowing clouds below us. Dusk was falling as we crossed the Channel above Boulogne and headed for Dungeness. And soon—incredibly soon—the myriad lights of London spread out below us, like some stupendous set-piece to herald journey's end. In a little over half an hour after leaving the French coast at Boulogne we were on the ground at Northolt.

A swift car bore me home; and my wife and son, greeting me in the hall, had one simultaneous query—a query tinged, I thought, with slight anxiety:

" Have they ' changed ' you? "

CHAPTER 8

Nerve-centre in a Mews

No, I had not been changed, though now that I was back in a normal environment I began to understand how it was that so many people fell under the spell of Caux. Almost everything there combines to stifle free thought. From the moment of arrival the average visitor is under the wing of one Buchmanite or another, and propaganda and ready-made slogans are pumped into his ear incessantly.

At Assemblies, or in the theatre, more ready-made ideas, often attractive, acceptable ideas, are similarly pumped into him. The calculated use of music and theme songs also helps to play upon his emotions, and thus makes him more receptive of those ideas. In addition to all this, the exhilaration of the mountain air and the imposing surroundings and the general atmosphere of good fellowship and cheerfulness all help to load the dice against anyone marked down for " change."

To be anything but cheerful and friendly and companionable in such an atmosphere is hardly possible. Thus one becomes abnormally tolerant—more receptive of other people's ideas. It is only by getting down to sea level again that some sense of proportion can be regained.

But I couldn't pretend to be able to form a balanced judgment yet. Back in London, I added the new data I had collected to the other material in my filing cabinet and wondered how I was ever going to sort it all out. I knew now why those Royal Commissions sit for years and never get anywhere. A truly exhaustive inquiry demands patience and persistence.

There were other claims on my time, too, for fresh assignments had to be tackled. Articles had to be written, and various commissions took me out of town. I might be in Leeds and Harrogate one week, and in Portsmouth and Southampton the next. Thus, my study of the Buchmanism dossiers had to be spasmodic.

However, by splitting the material into sections, under headings similar to those I had devised for tabulating the notes I jotted down in Switzerland, I gradually made headway. In the end I produced a 10,000-word report, covering " Present Activities," " Mountain House," " Assemblies," " Organization and Finances," " Propaganda," " College of the Good Road," " Evolution," and " Future Plans."

When this report had been digested by the editor for whom I had flown to Caux, I was commissioned to write two special articles, one dealing with the latest activities of the Oxford Group, the other describing personalities I had met during my inquiries. When I got down to the task of writing these articles I found that there were one or two gaps in my knowledge. So, after some reflection, I decided to go along to the Buchmanites' London headquarters to seek enlightenment.

Officially, the registered headquarters are given as 4, Hay's Mews, London, W.1. and no stranger, wandering through those old cobbled lanes behind Berkeley Square, could possibly suspect that such a quiet backwater is the nerve-centre of a powerful international movement. The only visible clue might be the number of smart streamlined cars to be seen there, though in view of the proximity of Berkeley Square these would most probably pass unnoticed.

Yet, behind an unassuming façade, scenes of great activity are enacted. I had found this out during the early stages of my inquiries, when I had persuaded Garth Lean to take me on a conducted tour of inspection.

I was given a glimpse of the Group's well-organized Book Department, which dispatches Buchmanite literature all over the world, besides selling sheet music and gramophone records of Moral Re-Armament theme songs. In the same building were various administrative offices, a small printing machine, and a travel bureau which arranges many of the trans-world journeys undertaken by Buchmanites and their guests.

Across the Mews were more administrative offices, including a reception room, telephone switchboards, and teleprinter installation for maintaining contact with Mountain House. This section, I found, was really the back of Dr Buchman's house, 45, Berkeley Square, with which it is linked by underground passage. A duel is said to have been fought in that passage in the days when the mansion above was the home of Clive of India. There is a legend that the ghosts of the duellists haunt it still, but the Buchmanites smile at that and have staked their own solid claim to the adjoining basement rooms.

As at Mountain House, all the administrative duties are carried out by volunteer workers. In fact, I was assured that the only paid staff consisted of cleaners and electricians, although they had all been " changed " and were now fervent Buchmanites themselves.

Clive's kitchen, in which old roasting spits and other relics are exhibited, serves as a canteen for the headquarters staff. It was there that I had tea with William Yates, the miner from North Staffordshire who, at our first meeting in Charles Street, offered to " walk back to Stoke " if it would convince me of his sincerity.

Another room has been converted into a modern kitchen where the volunteer cooks produce first-class meals; and lining the basement passage are huge store cupboards, stacked so high with good things that even if the flow of gifts ceased tomorrow the headquarters staff need not go hungry for a long, long time. One cupboard, crammed with scores of jars of fruit, was, Lean explained, the result of a home-bottling drive by some of their supporters.

He then led me through the passage and up into Dr Buchman's house, the gift of friends and supporters, and vested with the other buildings in the incorporated body of the Oxford Group.

Above the first flight of the broad staircase I noticed a fine oil painting of Dr Buchman by Frank O. Salisbury. It depicted the American in early middle age, wearing a fashionably-cut dark suit with a faint chalk stripe. His right hand, hanging by his side, clutched a slim blue volume; his left hand was thrust casually into his trouser pocket. A sagging watch-chain indicated the beginnings of a paunch. The face was thoughtful, a little sad; but highlights on forehead and glasses lent the features radiance. It was a striking painting, but it might have been the portrait of a prosperous business man—the director, say, of a big store, or a Building Society.

I passed through suites of rooms used for conferences or for conducting personal interviews. In one of these, Lean told me, Peter Howard had written some of his best-selling books on Buchmanism. I also inspected the main reception hall, which had been adapted during the war years as a makeshift theatre for the presentation of Moral Re-Armament plays. It was here, too, that the Buchmanites held their famous luncheon and dinner-parties at which their leader always insisted upon crowding in a maximum number of guests.

He had worked it out that by laying the places very closely together, the oval table could be made to accommodate twenty-one people. Some of his younger followers didn't share this enthusiasm for crowds, for being crammed in elbow to elbow meant eating under difficulties.

A story is told that during one of Buchman's temporary absences someone discovered a spare leaf to that oval table. Joyfully a little party of conspirators decided to insert that extra leaf and say nothing about it. On their leader's return they preened themselves on the fact that at least they could sit down twenty-one strong with some degree of comfort. But before he had taken more than a few sips at his soup, Buchman blinked round through his glasses and observed brightly: " Do you know, I believe we could squeeze in twenty-four at this table, after all."

I liked that story, and I believed it to be true, for I knew from my own experience how his guests were always packed in.

Lying upon that oval table when I looked in was an album containing photographs and war records of Buchmanites who had served in the Forces during World War II. The cover bore ribbons of the decorations they had won. " Everything from the V.C. down ! " said Lean proudly.

* * *

It was on an afternoon early in October that I decided to revisit the Buchmanite headquarters, taking with me a copy of my background report and a note of the additional information I desired. I asked for Lean, but he was not yet back from Caux, so, in his absence, I was received by Captain Dilly, Director of Publications, and another Buchmanite, named Don Simpson. We ran over a number of points together, and when I left, it was with a promise that the additional facts I desired would be forthcoming within a few days.

Things moved swiftly after that. Three days later Captain Dilly telephoned me to say that Lean was due back in London that night and had sent a special invitation for me to dine with him at Charles Street. There were points he would like to discuss with me rather urgently. I said I was a little pressed, and suggested deferring the discussion until after the week-end.

" I think Lean would like to see you *before* then," said Captain Dilly. " Could you manage tomorrow? "

I told him that I was taking tomorrow off, as it was my birthday; but he seemed so persistent that I finally gave way and offered as a compromise to meet Lean's plane at Northolt and have a quick chat with him there.

But, for some reason or other, this alternative did not find favour.

" I know Lean specially wants you to come to dinner," insisted the Captain.

" All right," I capitulated. " I'll come."

That dinner party, I decided, as I replaced the receiver, promised to be interesting.

It was. Very interesting. But instead of developing as I expected it would do, it gave a completely new turn to events and opened up fresh ground for speculation on the ways of my Buchmanite hosts.

Surprise number one was the discovery on arrival that I was not the only guest. Mr Bernard M. Hallward, President of St Raymond Paper Ltd, of Montreal, was also there, having flown back with Lean from Caux. The moment he was introduced I placed him as the man who had made that Sunday morning appeal for three million francs. I remembered, too, that I had seen his name among Governors of the College of the Good Road. So I was in distinguished company.

The dinner, well up to Buchmanite standards, was served in a pleasant front room. Besides Lean and Hallward, Captain Dilly and Don Simpson were present. Conversation soon turned on my proposed articles, Lean explaining to Hallward the extraordinary pains I was taking in gathering my facts. They had both read my background notes and thought them remarkably detailed; but they were surprised that the Assemblies at Caux had not impressed me as much as they did most people.

When I remarked that those family " confessions " struck me as inappropriate for an international gathering of that character, Lean said, no; the nature of the Assemblies was always carefully schemed. Sometimes a whole meeting might be devised with the idea of presenting a " message " to one individual. It was, I gathered, rather like Hamlet's device of getting the players to re-enact the circumstances of his father's murder to bring it home to his uncle.

Hallward corroborated this by citing a case within his knowledge of a man whose son, a former drunkard, had been " changed " by the Buchmanites. They wanted to change the father, too, so they managed to induce him to attend one of their Assemblies, at which the son appeared on the platform to testify how he had been reclaimed. This tipped the scale with the father. " If it can do that for my son," he was reported to have said, " then it can help me, too."

I asked Hallward how he had first been attracted to the Group. His reply was graphic.

" It was when I first saw thirty happy people," he declared. " I'd never seen so many *genuinely* happy people in one bunch before. It made me feel I wanted to know *why* they were so cheerful."

This had been a good many years before, when Buchman had been touring Canada from coast to coast with a " task force." Hallward told me that he had gone along to the gathering in Montreal with some reluctance, but had been completely won over.

One of his first moves on being " changed " was to make restitution for something which had not previously troubled his conscience unduly. In his frequent travels he had been in the habit of evading Customs duty. This had gone on over a period of years.

" I sat down with pencil and paper and calculated the amount I owed," he explained in between mouthfuls of superb roast chicken. " Then I added interest; compound interest. The total was formidable; but I paid it, and felt better."

Since that time Hallward has supported the Oxford Group both financially and with personal service. He told me how he had travelled through Germany with the task force which presented *The Forgotten Factor* and *The Good Road* revue in the Ruhr. He couldn't understand why the critics had been so frigid to the revue when it was shown in London. Whenever he had seen it audiences had always been tremendously appreciative.

As for the lessons which Buchmanism tried to impart, they were not to be laughed at.

" Just try living up to the four absolutes," he said. " Try being absolutely honest or absolutely unselfish— even for a year. It's not easy! "

At about this juncture the sweet was carried in—apple pie and cream. And here was surprise number two, for the pie stood in the centre of a big dish, encircled by the device "HAPPY BIRTHDAY," picked out in cherries. Remembering that I had mentioned my birthday to Captain Dilly merely as an excuse for deferring this meeting, I felt a little embarrassed. But worse was to follow. When we adjourned to an upper room for coffee, a red carnation lay beside my cup.

" Is this intelligent anticipation? " asked Hallward, with a smile.

" I think it's something the women have thought up by themselves," answered Lean as he proceeded to fasten the carnation in my lapel.

I accepted this demonstration with the best grace I could muster, though it was obvious that I was being fêted deliberately. It seemed all part of a calculated " softening-up " process, but whereas in war the weapons used for preliminary bombardment are guns or bombs, my hosts were using flattery and studied kindness. I felt like " Mr Anyman " in *The Good Road,* facing the honeyed onslaught of the forces of materialism! I was outnumbered four-to-one, remember.

As we sipped our coffee I had to listen to a lot of soft soap. Lean praised my background report as " masterly " and a " monumental production." He kept harping on this to the company till I began to squirm in my chair. " He must have a marvellous memory," he told his colleagues. " I was there, you know, when certain things were said by certain people. I saw no note taken, yet here everything is, all flicked into place in the report! It's astonishing."

There was a lot more in the same vein, and I tried to turn the conversation on to the subject of checking the report for any inaccuracies or misinterpretations which might have crept in. But it was futile.

" We don't want to go into that tonight," said Lean. " Come along on Monday morning at eleven and have coffee with us, and if there's anything to clear up we can do it then."

I took my leave at last after effusive farewells, Captain Dilly volunteering to drive me to Baker Street in his car. As we were going out Lean came rushing down the stairs to press a package into my hand.

" Something from Switzerland! " he said. It was a packet of milk chocolate.

* * *

On the Monday morning I received a telephone message changing my morning coffee engagement into a date for afternoon tea. I was glad of the few extra hours' respite in which to ponder on the new situation. A title of some improving book of childhood's days flashed across my mind—*Wild Nature Won by Kindness*. It was patent now that the Buchmanites were wooing me; hoping by soft words and kindness to gain, if not my esteem, at least my sympathy. There could be only one interpretation of this. They must have found my background notes a little too detailed for their peace of mind.

Had I made a mistake in trying to probe too deeply? After all, I had only been asked to write two articles, and I had more than sufficient material for those. However, having committed myself to further inquiries, I was determined to see them through. I was also determined to adopt a firm attitude with those men at Charles Street. On the way to keep the appointment that afternoon I rehearsed in my mind exactly what I intended to say. I would be brief but candid, and preface the interview with some such words as these:

" Look here, gentlemen, I appreciate all the hospitality and kindness you have shown me, but let's get this straight: I'm only doing a job and trying to be fair to everybody—so please let's be quite frank about it and cut out the soft soap and flattery and get down to business in a straightforward way. I've shown you my personal notes, which I would hardly have done if I hadn't been sincere. If I've misinterpreted any facts, please put me right. I want to try to present the truth. But we can't get at the truth if we have any more play-acting."

It has been my experience in life that most rehearsed speeches of this kind get left unsaid; and this little effort at candour proved no exception. For I sensed, as soon as I was ushered upstairs for tea with Dilly and Lean, that a completely different atmosphere prevailed. There was no effusiveness; no attempt at flattery; no soft soap. So half my prepared speech was rendered superfluous at once. Then Lean announced that he had been through my report and had prepared some notes thereon which he thought we might run over together.

" Mind you," he said, " my notes are only suggestions; what you yourself feel or write is purely a matter for you."

With this reasonable overture the remainder of my contemplated " speech " was made unnecessary. It seemed odd that not so many hours before, in this very room, Lean had pinned that carnation in my buttonhole to the accompaniment of flattering phrases. The Buch-manites had turned a somersault. Perhaps they had realized that the ceremonies of that night had been over-done? I was glad they were now in a sensible frame of mind.

Immediately after tea the three of us drew up our chairs to a table and got down to work in earnest. We ran through my thirty-page report section by section while Lean, with his notes before him, made his observations. His first consideration was to bring me up to date, for a lot had happened in the weeks which had elapsed since I had left Caux. The figure of visiting delegates had risen from 5,000 from seventy-one countries to 8,000 from eighty-two countries.

He had also provided some helpful notes about per-sonalities among the latest arrivals—men like the Member of Parliament for Nagasaki, and a Member of the Senate for Hiroshima; Lord Hinchingbrooke, Sir Stanley Reed, MP; George Villiers, President of the Employers' Association of France, and Hussein Bey Fahmy, Egyptian Minister of Finance. Then there was a goodwill message in which Dr Karl Arnold, Minister-President of North Rhine-Westphalia, Germany, and four fellow Ministers pledged their readiness to work together with Moral Re-Armament.

When all new material had been disposed of, Lean came to a criticism which he said had been raised by Bernard Hallward. This concerned the use of certain words in my report which " during the last few years have obtained a derogatory flavour among the general public."

One of these, it seemed, was " propaganda." It was felt that people's memories of Dr Goebbels were too fresh for them to dissociate the use of propaganda plays and propaganda songs from Nazi publicity methods. They were sensitive, too, about my use of the word " showmanship " in a paragraph dealing with the way in which the Assemblies were stage-managed. And they thought " chorus " would be better than " choir " as a description of their massed singers because people might remember Aimée Semple McPherson and her " angels."

Then the question of family " confessions," which we had discussed at dinner that night, came up again. Lean insisted that : " These simple stories of honesty, far from being inappropriate, are often the keys to new effectiveness for the families, and so for the public lives, of the statesmen present." He reiterated his statement that such simple stories were " put on for a specific purpose to help specific people."

Next came a correction of one of his own facts. He had told me that the European circulation of the Moral Re-Armament magazine *New World News* was 50,000 copies. He now said this represented world-wide sale.

There were other notes of no great importance, but one in reply to a special query I had raised was decidedly interesting. Remarking upon the Oxford Group's fluid constitution, I had asked if this might not prove dangerous now that it was pitting itself against Communism—an ideology noted for its skill at infiltration.

Having no system of enrolment, and no system of registration for its followers, the Group, I held, could

K

never be sure who was sincerely " changed " or who was professing change merely to get into the movement. It had cells in every country; so had the Communists. How could it possibly prevent infiltration by any ill-disposed political opponents who might have ideas about seizing the Buchmanites' wealth and converting the organization to their own ends?

I argued that this was not as fantastic as it might sound at first. What I had seen at Caux had shown me that followers of MRA were already living a form of voluntary Communism, eradicating class barriers, racial barriers, sharing everything, favouring a communal existence, and forming themselves into voluntary labour squads to perform all necessary chores.

Lean had prepared a written reply to this poser. Here it is:

> As a matter of fact, we never have been infiltrated—which is more than can be said, for example, of the Canadian Government or our own Civil Service.
> I think one reason is because we have an active ideology, which means that people have to live out the four standards of absolute honesty, purity, unselfishness and love. This is difficult to fake.
> It is a well-known psychological fact that living on these standards greatly sharpens your diagnosis of yourself and other people. All our experienced workers are fairly cute at spotting motives.
> Of course, great care is taken before anybody is selected to speak at a place like Caux, and even greater care and a considerable period of probation is necessary before anyone becomes a whole-time worker. This is a considerable safeguard.

In one way or another, then, that afternoon conference was fairly fruitful. It dissipated the artificial atmosphere of that dinner party, provided me with a number of new facts, and cleared up a number of minor misunderstandings. My articles would be all the stronger in consequence.

*   *   *

I thought I had paid my last visit to Charles Street, but a few days later Captain Dilly telephoned and invited me to lunch. No special reason was advanced to account for this invitation, but I thought I might as well go along in case Dilly or Lean had some afterthoughts to add to points we had thrashed out at our last conference. As it happened, they had nothing, and the luncheon was not marked by any special discussions that I can remember.

Most of our conversation, I believe, was of a general character, though my hosts inquired closely as to the progress I was making with my articles. In view of the contact we had maintained throughout my protracted investigation, their curiosity seemed natural enough. They said they were eager to see the articles in print and asked if any publication date had been fixed. I told them I thought the first might appear towards the end of November.

My articles were, in fact, written and delivered, but I had not yet seen proofs. I was busy on other work now —commissions for two stories for children's annuals and some feature articles which took me out of town for two or three days.

In my absence, my first Caux article was scheduled for a certain issue of the magazine which had commissioned it, and a decision being taken to run it into a section printed in full colour, the question of illustrations arose. I had handed in a selection of black-and-white pictures with my copy, but, in his quest for colour photographs, the art editor contacted the Buchmanite headquarters. Of course, they promised full co-operation.

Thus, I arrived home to find that Lean had been telephoning me there and had left a message asking me to ring him up as soon as convenient. I did so, and found him anxious about the request for colour pictures. They had a big selection to offer, but some were in Caux and others were in America. Could we wait until they were obtained? I said we could, and gave him a final date on which they must be in our hands. He promised we should have them by then; and that promise was duly kept.

Arising out of these negotiations over pictures came another pressing luncheon invitation. This proved to be a slightly larger gathering, for Mrs Lean presided as hostess, and besides her husband, Dilly and myself, a fifth person appeared, a Mr William Jaeger, who had been actively associated with the Oxford Group for many years.

We had barely taken our seats when Lean fired what I thought a rather curious question in my direction. "What is the general impression of Press people about the Group?" he asked. "What do they really think of us? Do they think the Oxford Group is some kind of cult—or what?"

I had to confess that I couldn't answer that one. I had read numerous articles, of course, but they had always seemed a trifle vague. In fact, I had been led to the conclusion that nobody had ever taken the trouble of trying to find out what its true purpose was."

"They're the queer ones," said Mr Jaeger across the table. "We're not queer! But people can't see that!"

He went on very eloquently to sketch the aims and objects of Buchmanism, by which I was reminded of a book I had brought along for Lean. It was the *Autobiography of Benjamin Franklin*, and in its pages I had found what might almost have been a blue-print for Buchmanism.

I mentioned this now and told them how Franklin had devised a "great and extensive project" as a result of an intensive study of history. He had noted that wars and revolutions were carried on by parties, whose different views occasioned all confusion. He had observed, too, that while a party was preoccupied with its general design, individual members had their particular private interests in view. Then, as soon as a party gained its general objective, each member would become intent upon his personal interest, which would lead to division and confusion all over again.

From these reflections Franklin had reached the conclusion that few men in public affairs really acted for the good of their country. Their actions might bring good, but they did not act from benevolence, but because they considered their own interests united with that of their country. " Fewer still," he had written, " act with a view to the good of mankind."

" When you read the remedy he proposed for all this, I think you'll be as surprised as I was," I said.

Lean reached out in a flash and grabbed the book from a side table.

" Come on, then," he said, handing it to me. " Suppose you read it aloud—then we can all hear it."

Feeling a little self-conscious, I found the place and started to read :

> "There seems to me at present to be a great occasion for raising a United Party for Virtue, by forming the virtuous and good men of all nations into a regular body, to be governed by suitable good and wise rules, which good and wise men may probably be more unanimous in their obedience to, than common people are to common laws.
>
> "I at present think that whoever attempts this aright, and is well qualified, can not fail of pleasing God, and of meeting with success. . . ."

I looked round the table to see the effect these words were having upon the others. They betrayed no sign.

" Go on," said Lean.

> "I was not discouraged by the seeming magnitude of the undertaking [I read]. As I have always thought that one man of tolerable abilities may work great *changes*, and accomplish great affairs among mankind, if he first forms a good plan, and, cutting off all amusements or other employments that would divert his attention, makes the execution of that same plan his sole study and business."

Much to my surprise, there was no great show of interest in this disclosure that a great figure in American history had undoubtedly thought of " Moral Re-Armament " nearly two hundred years ago. Apparently for them there was no prophet but Frank Buchman! Ben Franklin could go hang.

That was the last time I lunched at Charles Street.

*   *   *

But it was not the last I was to hear of the Buchmanites. A few days before my first article was to appear I opened a rival magazine to find that it contained a full-page article on the World Assembly at Caux. I had been " scooped."

That was bad enough in itself, but there was poison on the barb. It was the Buchmanites who had " scooped " me, for the article was signed by their prize convert—Peter Howard.

CHAPTER 9

What's Behind It All?

WHY had they done this thing? Why had they chosen to show their hand so crudely? What could have moved them to be so indiscreet as to perpetrate a tactical blunder of this kind? A blunder it undoubtedly was, for it immediately betrayed their weakness.

" All our experienced workers are fairly cute," Lean had written only a few days before. Perhaps they thought it a " cute " move to publish their own evaluation of Caux in a rival magazine in the same week that the first of my own articles was due to appear? Yet I could hardly think them so foolish as that.

Anyway, whatever their intention, their very action was tantamount to an admission that they could not face independent comment. Their article was plainly intended as a counterblast to anything that I might write. What had they to fear?

I combed Peter Howard's article for anything that would bring me fresh enlightenment. I combed in vain. Most of what he had written was familiar stuff which I had read repeatedly in the Group's own propaganda sheets. Naturally, he sought to make the most of the Caux Assembly as an event of immense international importance. Some distinguished delegates were named, and there was the inevitable quotation from Dr Buchman:

> Moral Re-Armament gives the full dimension of change. Economic change. Social change. National change. International change. All based on personal change. It creates a personal opinion adequate to remake the world.

And yet, if the article seemed stale propaganda to me,

I had to acknowledge the Group's amazing ingenuity and application in launching this attempt to take the wind out of my sails. It must, I reflected, have demanded a great deal of careful pre-planning and no small amount of persuasion to induce the proprietors of a big weekly to accept a propaganda article and to publish it in a specific issue.

That alone was evidence of the Group's influence. I thought I had plumbed Group affairs pretty deeply, but this new manifestation of its methods showed me that I had still a lot to learn.

My articles occasioned considerable attention, and letters poured in from all over the country for several weeks.

One was from Thomas Powell, the ex-strike leader, who was full of praise for all he had seen at Caux. He had been especially impressed by the College of the Good Road.

Scores of other letters I recognized as coming from Buchmanites or Buchmanite supporters, and the extra-ordinary thing was that they ignored my criticisms and wrote in eulogistic terms. Many writers thanked me for my fairness and accuracy. Some said I had given them a deeper knowledge of the work of the Group and its leaders. Others expressed gratitude for " the plain presentation of facts, and the absence of fictitious stories such as have in the past been used to deride this movement."

One curious phenomenon was the arrival of two different letters signed by the same person, one dated from a London club, the other from a Devon hotel. Both expressed thanks for my articles in different terms. The writer, I discovered, was a member of the Council of Management of the Oxford Group! Another whole-time worker whom I knew to be employed in the London head-quarters also wrote in, his letter being posted in Northern Ireland.

All things considered, it struck me that I was merely on the threshold of the Group's mysteries. So, although my commission for the magazine was completed, I decided to continue my probe. My curiosity was far from sated.

*   *   *

I felt that the only thing to do was to go back to the beginning, examine the Group's early history much more closely than I had done so far, and try, if possible, to trace its evolution up to the present time.

One thing which prompted me to take this course was a growing conviction that there was some kind of cleavage somewhere. At Caux, and in all the literature issued there, the term MRA or Moral Re-Armament seemed to figure exclusively. Yet in a lot of the printed matter I had gathered together in London the term Oxford Group was favoured.

I had noted, too, that there was much more mention of religion when the Oxford Group was involved, and much more talk of politics where Moral Re-Armament was concerned. I knew that the organization's London registration was "The Oxford Group," while the Swiss registration was "Fondation du Réarmement Morale." It was all very puzzling.

It would have been simple to have gone back to the London headquarters with fresh lists of questions, but I preferred to delve for myself. I therefore began to re-comb all the material I had collected, paying special attention to anything which had any bearing on the Group's history.

The account which Loudon Hamilton had given me of Dr Buchman's first descent upon Oxford served as an excellent starting point. He had told me how undergraduates had queued up for a chance to chat with the American for a few moments, and how interest had spread rapidly through the whole university.

From *Life Changers* by the late Harold Begbie, I gleaned a detailed picture of how Buchman's influence had developed. At that time, Buchman was publicity-shy and, learning that Begbie contemplated writing a book, he offered co-operation only on condition that his own name did not appear. Consequently, his identity is thinly masked throughout by the use of the initials " F. B."

Thinking of the scenes I had witnessed at Caux, I found this revelation of Buchman's early modesty decidedly interesting. It is quite evident, from Begbie's account, that politics or big-scale showmanship were far from Buchman's thoughts in those early days at Oxford. Although he held what were termed " house-parties " at which young men were moved to stand up and confess to past misdemeanours, he was chiefly concerned with practising a unique form of personal evangelism.

But tales about those house-parties spread and gave rise to rumours. There was talk of exhibitionism, and some Buchmanites say today that stories were fabricated by a malicious person. Yet Begbie makes it clear that confessions of sexual aberrations figured largely in the cases dealt with privately by Buchman. He cites instance upon instance of young men unbosoming themselves to the American concerning their temptations and their lapses, sometimes talking till two in the morning. They found his counsel comforting.

But some of these men, it seems, spoke " with troubled criticism of their leader, disliking some of his pet phrases, disapproving as vigorously as I did of his theological opinions, but all sticking to him with an unconquerable loyalty as the man who had worked a great miracle in their lives, and who was by far the most remarkable man of their experience in spite of everything that troubled their taste or their judgment."

The operative word there, it seems to me, is " experience." As undergraduates it could not have been very extensive!

Begbie himself confesses to disappointment and disapproval in those early days.

> I did not like the manner in which the early discussions were conducted [he writes in his preface]. Many of the phrases used in describing a really unique religious experience seemed to me second-hand and unconvincing; I could not help feeling that I was not merely wasting my time, but that I was foolishly permitting my nerves to be unprofitably irritated.

However, that phase seems to have passed as larger " house-parties " were arranged and the circle of followers became too big for private consultations to be maintained. Public confessions appear to have continued, but so far as I have been able to gather, they were mostly of a trivial nature. A cook might confess to having cheated her mistress over the housekeeping accounts; a young ward might confess to having helped herself to biscuits from the sideboard while her guardian was out of the room.

But, side by side with this sort of thing, a more serious-minded nucleus of young men devoted themselves to the task of spreading the Christian religion. The Oxford Group had yet to be born. They were known then as " A First-century Christian Fellowship."

Their work proceeded under that banner for eight years. Then seven of their number, some of them Rhodes Scholars, made a resolve to spend their long vacation in propagating their spiritual experiences in South Africa. It was on that tour that they first became known as " The Oxford Group."

Accounts of how that happened vary. Some say the christening was done by the South African newspapers; others favour a more picturesque explanation, and say that, during their travels, a coloured porter, hearing that they were a group of passengers from Oxford, chalked " Oxford Group " on their car as a means of identification.

Whichever version is true, it is certain that the new title dates from 1928, though it was not registered officially until eleven years later.

The success achieved by the small group of pioneers led Buchman to visit the Union of South Africa in 1929 with nineteen picked workers. A three months' campaign was conducted, and in the following year an even larger party was sent out.

In 1932–3–4 the Oxford Groupers, steadily growing in numbers, visited Canada, making a coast-to-coast tour. They seem to have made quite an impression, for the then Prime Minister, the Rt Hon R. B. Bennett, declared that their influence had been felt " in every village and city, even in the remotest outposts of the Dominion," and that their work had made the task of government easier.

The accent was still on religion. The first Moderator of the United Church of Canada spoke of their tour as " by all odds the greatest spiritual movement in the history of Canada, which has set fire to the whole country and brought to fruition the work of the Church."

Then, on their return to England, the Archbishop of Canterbury, the late Cosmo Lang, commissioned Dr Buchman and 100 of the Oxford Group whole-time workers, at Lambeth Palace, for evangelistic work in London. On October 7, 1933, usually remembered as the year in which Hitler came to power, 7,000 people attended a public commissioning service conducted in St Paul's Cathedral by the then Bishop of London, Winnington Ingram.

And shortly after that the Archbishop told his clergy: " This Group is certainly doing what the Church of Christ exists everywhere to do; it is changing human lives."

Reviewing facts like these, I could hardly refrain from comparing the programme of those days with the contrasting scenes I had witnessed at Caux. The Group at that time was twelve years old, but there was still no hint of political ambitions or of "moral re-armament." It seemed to be functioning chiefly as an auxiliary to the Church.

While the campaign was proceeding in London, the President of the Norwegian Parliament, the Hon C. J. Hambro, then on a visit to our own House of Commons, invited the Group to go to Norway.

In the following summer, speaking at Oxford, Buchman proclaimed his aims in the following terms:

"The Oxford Group is a Christian revolution whose concern is vital Christianity. Its aim is a new social order under the dictatorship of the spirit of God, making for better human relationships, for unselfish co-operation, for cleaner business, for cleaner politics, for the elimination of political, industrial and racial antagonisms. World-changing will come through life-changing."

No one could quarrel with that or say that it was not explicit. People could no longer ask what the Group was supposed to be after. The leader had defined its programme with admirable clarity.

Northern Ireland was visited next for a two months' campaign. Then, in response to that invitation made in the preceding year, the Group sent thirty picked workers to Norway.

Their triumph there was phenomenal. Mr Hambro had asked about 100 of his friends to meet the visitors, but ten times that number turned up. Then, when meetings were held in Oslo, they attracted more than 24,000 people. Bishop Berggrav, later Primate of the Church of Norway, declared the effect to be "the greatest spiritual movement since the Reformation."

In the following spring the Group launched a campaign in Denmark with an international team 300 strong. A demonstration attended by 10,000 was held in Hamlet's Castle of Elsinore.

That autumn, on the eve of the Danish general election, 23,000 people crowded Copenhagen's largest hall and the cathedral for a Group meeting, under Danish leadership, and called for all parties to submit national policy to divine guidance. "It is beyond question that our country has never before experienced the irresistible power of such a religious tide," said the Press next day.

On the anniversary of the Group's first visit to Denmark meetings were held all over the country. "A new road to the old Gospel, that is my conception of the Oxford Group," declared the Primate. "Christ the Saviour, the Saviour of the world and of the individual soul: that is the message of the Oxford Group."

And so, with the accent still on religion, the Group extended its work. But a climacteric was approaching. War clouds were gathering, millions of lives were destined to be changed inexorably, and the Group itself was about to enter upon a new phase.

As the threat of World War II loomed nearer and nations embarked upon an armaments race, Buchman, ever an opportunist, seized that moment for launching something entirely new—Moral Re-Armament. That was in May 1938; and the place was East Ham Town Hall.

Two months before Hitler had marched into Austria, the "war of nerves" was at its height. A crowd of 3,000 had flocked to hear Dr Buchman. This is what he said:-

"The world's condition cannot but cause disquiet and anxiety. Hostility piles up between nation and nation, labour and capital, class and class. The cost of bitterness and fear mounts daily. Friction and frustration are undermining our homes.

"Is there a remedy that will cure the individual and the nation and give the hope of a speedy and satisfactory recovery?

" The remedy may lie in a return to those simple home truths that some of us learned at our mother's knee, and which many of us have forgotten and neglected—honesty, purity, unselfishness and love.

" The crisis is fundamentally a moral one. The nations must re-arm morally. Moral recovery is essentially the forerunner of economic recovery."

He went on to tell something of his philosophy of life-changing. " God alone can change human nature. The secret lies in that great forgotten truth that when man listens, God speaks; when man obeys, God acts; when men change, nations change."

Then, after applying his philosophy to industrial problems, and repeating some of his old slogans like: " Suppose everybody cared enough, everybody shared enough, wouldn't everybody have enough " and " There is enough in the world for everyone's need, but not for everyone's greed," he worked up to a forceful peroration: " We can, we must, and we will generate a moral and spiritual force that is powerful enough to remake the world."

His timing could hardly have been more perfect. Thousands must have felt that the idea was attractive, even if their common sense told them that tanks and bombers could not be stopped by idealism alone.

But Buchman knew that he had coined a phrase which would make all his past ideas seem like mottoes out of a Christmas cracker. " Moral Re-Armament " was the thing from now on! Fired by this knowledge, he cheerfully adapted old slogans. Where once he had said: " Labour led by God will lead the world," he now declared: " A Nation led by God will lead the world." The Oxford Group was committed to a new phase.

On the same day in which he launched Moral Re-Armament, Buchman gave a talk to East London families in which he said: "Britain and the world must re-arm morally. God gave me this as a key thought for this year specially. God will be in charge of these Isles. Somebody has got to start. Will you be that person? Forget all about Frank Buchman, and that one day he had a quiet time and now you have a movement in fifty-two countries. Otherwise, you will miss the point of all this.

"This is my birthday message to you. Why have we been so long learning this? The only sane people in an insane world are those guided by God. Is East London going to bring the world back to sanity?"

Buchman was then sixty, and so energetic that in the same year he attended assemblies at Visby, Sweden, Interlaken, Geneva, and again in London. Inspired by his newly-found "Moral Re-Armament" idea, he made speech after speech. "Moral Re-Armament creates white and red corpuscles, energy and protection, in the national blood stream," he told an audience at Interlaken. "The poisons of decadence and division are thrown off, as a healthy organism throws off disease."

Undoubtedly 1938 was one of Buchman's most fruitful years. Flushed with his new triumphs, he decided in the spring of 1939 to launch Moral Re-Armament in America. This decision was a fateful one, and it was destined to alter the whole trend of Buchmanism.

For, when war came, Buchman was still in America and with him were some thirty British followers who elected to remain at his side. They were not to see England again for seven years, and in those seven years strange "changes" indeed were to take place in their organization. And all because of that clever phrase "Moral Re-Armament."

*   *   *

Studying the wartime developments in Buchmanism in America, I came to understand the significance of

The Good Road depicts a modern Pilgrim's Progress, and here "Madame Lust" whispers blandishments in the ear of "Mr Anyman" in an effort to seduce him from the straight and narrow path. "Greed," "Fear," "Confusion," and "Hate" look on, hoping for his downfall.

A highlight in an industrial sketch in The Good Road. Miss Trust (clad entirely in red) sows seeds

something which the Oxford Group's secretary, Roland Wilson, had said to me when I was questioning him so relentlessly on that drive from Lausanne to Caux. " Dr Buchman's genius," he had said, " lies in the way in which he has constantly rearticulated his message to meet the need of the hour."

There can be no doubt that Buchman gave this genius full rein when he tackled the problem of " selling " Moral Re-Armament to the American public.

With Europe on the brink of World War II and with the United States certain to be drawn in sooner or later, it would have been fatuous to have presented his new code as the one sure specific for peace. Lesser men might have wilted and turned to something else; but Buchman did not falter.

He knew that he had coined the phrase of a lifetime, and he did not intend to let it die. With characteristic shrewdness he made an all-out effort to identify his Group's interests with those of the United States. A new word began to creep into the Group's vocabulary. That word was *patriotism*.

Meetings were organized in Washington, New York, and Los Angeles to present " a new pattern for Democracy." In Washington Buchman struck the keynote.

" We need a new dedication of our people to the elementary virtues of honesty, unselfishness and love; and we must have the will again to find what unites people rather than what divides them. It must become the dawn of a new era, a new age, a new civilization. The future depends not only on what a few men may decide to do in Europe, but upon what a million men decide to be in America."

How well he understood the American public.

That summer the University of Oglethorpe conferred upon him the honorary degree of Doctor of Laws. He

L

seized the opportunity for asking the students: "What will happen to America if war comes to Europe? If, as Emerson suggests, America is God's last chance to make a world, then we have to have a different America. . . . The function of universities in a world crisis is to create new men who can fashion the new civilization. . . . America can give a whole new pattern to civilization. The time is over-ripe. We must change and give a world-wide message with a national voice."

It was all so sensible, besides being flattering to his hearers. But this was merely the prelude. A month later a crowd of 45,000 flocked to hear him speak at the Holly-wood Bowl, 15,000 of them having to be turned away. A tremendous spectacle was provided, with four search-light beams stabbing the Californian sky to represent the four Absolutes—absolute honesty, absolute purity, absolute unselfishness, and absolute love. And this is how Buchman introduced Moral Re-Armament to the multitude:

"Moral Re-Armament is the scenario of a Golden Age—a God-directed production—a preview of a New World. Hollywood, that goes to every home, can become the sounding board for Moral Re-Armament to the nations. . . . MRA will win, because it advances with the strength of a united mind, because it awakens the fire of true patriotism. . . ."

A World Assembly on the Monterey Peninsula followed. "The choice is 'Guidance or Guns?'" he said in his opening address, cheerfully adapting Goering's well-known 'Guns-before-butter' quip. "We must listen to guidance or we will listen to guns."

Two months later the guns began to roar in Europe, and in a world broadcast from San Francisco, Buchman declared: "The way to outlive the forces of destruction is to build better and more wisely than we are building now. . . . Our instant need is for millions to plan for the new world."

He heralded 1940 with a special New Year's message:

> For America this year is a year of destiny. We have the opportunity of giving the pattern for a new world. Our task is to enlist everyone in America's war—the war for industrial co-operation and national unity. . . . Will America be the builder of the foundations for a new world?

And, broadcasting in the summer of the same year, he said:

> True preparedness—the result of a nation morally re-armed— is the responsibility of every citizen. . . . The eleventh hour has struck for America. America can no longer be lulled into a false sense of security by dreaming of the sweet by-and-by. We must face the nasty now-and-now.

In the following year it was: "Moral Re-Armament is a message of the highest patriotism. It gives every American the chance to play his part."

And he spoke of MRA's "patriotic dramatizations," "this far-reaching patriotic service," and characterized MRA workers as "patriots who have been fighting daily over long periods."

He was at the peak of his form at this period, often showing a shrewdness and vision which a top-flight statesman might well have envied. I shall have more to say of that in a later chapter, but the extracts I have given here indicate the persistence with which he planted the idea of Moral Re-Armament in American soil.

While he was thus engaged in explaining "the true patriotism" to the masses, his followers were actively engaged in producing bulk quantities of propaganda to match up with his new interpretation of MRA. Books, pamphlets, plays, and musicals were devised in succession. There was even a MRA National Defence Handbook which, with the winning title *You Can Defend America,* and a foreword by General Pershing, achieved a circulation of 1,350,000 copies.

This was followed up promptly with a "War Revue" bearing the same title, which toured through twenty States and played to audiences totalling 250,000. Another version, called *Pull Together Canada*, was launched across the 49th Parallel to audiences of miners, steelworkers, shipyard workers, and their families.

The MRA Training Centre—forerunner of Mountain House, Caux—was opened at Mackinac Island, Michigan, and Buchman, after some penetrating observations on Communism and Fascism, declared that America must discover her rightful ideology. "The battle for America is the battle for the mind of America," he said.

So far as he was concerned, he had already won that battle. He had not only captured the public's imagination, but had also won the backing of many public men who recognized that all this was helping to stimulate America's war effort.

Like it or not, Buchman's genius for "rearticulating his message" had certainly triumphed. MRA was established.

* * *

Meanwhile, Buchmanites in England, missing all the excitement of that amazing campaign, were having to face up to the realities of war. Most of their younger men were in the Services, but a nucleus remained in the "Citadel" in Berkeley Square. There, for their own amusement and the entertainment of their friends or fellow Buchmanites who might be passing through London on leave, they rigged up a theatre and staged MRA plays and musicals.

At the same time they strove to keep in step with their Transatlantic brothers by introducing patriotism into their programme. Early in the war they issued, through the civic heads of 550 cities and towns, a *Call to Our Citizens,* which began:

> Today, when our whole world is thre.. .ned with ruin, we feel more urgently than ever before the need for that new force of Moral Re-Armament which can create a new world, a world of sanity and order, a world of plenty and of peace. . . .

This was followed up during 1940–1 by an MRA morale leaflet. Then, as a counterpart to the *You Can Defend America* pamphlet, they produced *Battle Together for Britain,* first as a handbook, then as a revue. They also toured Army camps with a play called *Giant Otherfellow.*

At this time Peter Howard began writing his best-selling Moral Re-Armament books. In all, the Buchmanites in England claimed that they distributed 5,000,000 books and pamphlets during the war.

* * *

But their horizon was not altogether unclouded. Some people remembered that Buchman had once been quoted as saying: " I thank heaven for a man like Adolf Hitler " and had shown pro-German tendencies. Others made slighting comments about the party of eager young men of military age who were working with Buchman in the States and making no effort to return to their own country to " Battle Together for Britain." They were said to have had their permits extended repeatedly, and one highly placed American officer went so far as to say: " I regard this group of registrants as the most detestable specimens of draft-dodgers which have yet come to my attention."

In the House of Commons, too, when the question of deferment for Oxford Groupists was under discussion, Mr Ernest Bevin, then Minister of Labour and National Service, said: " Within the meaning of the National Service Act and their liability to serve their country, I am not prepared to accept the Oxford Group as a religious organization."

All these controversies might well have been forgotten long ago, for there was nothing very serious in them. But, foolishly, I think, the Buchmanites themselves have chosen to perpetuate them in a ninety-five page booklet entitled *The Fight to Serve*. In *Innocent Men*, too, Peter Howard rushed to the defence of Groupers whose eligibility for war service was in question, pointing out quite gravely that there were many reserved occupations—" ladies' corset-makers," for instance.

The official answer to the pro-German charge is that Dr Buchman was not fully quoted. Their version is as follows:

> I thank heaven for a man like Adolf Hitler who built a front line of defence against the anti-Christ of Communism. My barber in London told me Hitler saved all Europe from Communism. That's how he felt. Of course, I don't condone everything the Nazis do. Anti-Semitism? Bad, naturally. I suppose Hitler sees a Karl Marx in every Jew.
> But think what it would mean to the world if Hitler surrendered to the control of God. Or Mussolini. Or any dictator. Through such a man God could control a nation overnight and solve every bewildering problem.

So far as the English Buchmanites who were in America during the war are concerned, there is convincing evidence that their work was regarded as valuable by many of the United States authorities. There were only twenty-nine of them and those who were of military age and fit were ultimately drafted into the American forces, anyway.

In England, Mr Ernest Bevin's attitude certainly brought forth a great storm of protest from the Churches, and it is hard to see why the Group did not rest content when it had the championship of the Archbishops of Canterbury and York?

Its decision to give permanency to these stale wartime " scandals " may have method in it, though. It claims to have sold 155,000 copies of *Innocent Men*, and doubtless, at one shilling a copy, *The Fight to Serve* has likewise shown a handsome profit.

*   *   *

On the eve of returning to Europe in the spring of 1946, Buchman bade farewell to New York as follows: "We are at the end of seven years—seven wonderful years. We have learned much. . . . When I left England a great statesman said: 'I don't want you to leave my country. I want you to stay.' I said, 'My duty is to America. . . .'"

Having done his duty to America, Buchman returned to his Berkeley Square mansion, being greeted by a "Welcome Song," specially written for the occasion. And on June 4, his birthday, he was presented with a book containing more than a thousand names of people who had bought the Westminster Theatre for showing Moral Re-Armament plays and as a memorial to those who had died in the war.

In July 1946 the first World Assembly for Moral Re-Armament to be held in Europe since the war, was staged at Mountain House, Caux. It was attended by 2,500 people from twenty-six nations. Since then Assemblies have been held there yearly, steadily growing in size and scope, and with the anti-Communist note being sounded more strongly every year.

Such, briefly, is the history of the Oxford Group.

What of the men behind it?

CHAPTER 10

Men and Methods

As more and more pieces of my jig-saw puzzle fall into place a suggestion of a picture becomes discernible. I seem to see a bridge with two arches, one labelled " Oxford Group—Religion "; the other labelled " MRA —Politics." The supporting piers are identifiable, too. The first is marked "World War I," that in the centre is "World War II," and the third is " Fear of World War III." That central pier makes a clear-cut division in the evolution of Buchmanism. *For the first seventeen years of its life there was no mention of Moral Re-Armament.*

For the past fifteen years there has been little mention of Oxford Group. Today it seems as if it takes second place in importance. Indeed, when I mentioned Oxford Group in conversation with most of the people I met at Caux, it failed to register. To some people it appeared to convey little or nothing.

But it is not only the younger generation which thinks in terms of Moral Re-Armament. I found to my surprise that some of those who have been associated with Buchmanism from those first days at Oxford thought and talked of nothing but MRA, with the accent more acutely on world politics than on religion.

I have mentioned the fact that the Swiss Buchmanites call themselves the " Fondation du Réarmement Morale." That in itself is significant. All the literature on sale at Caux, too, is devoted to MRA. Delegates who go on the platform at Mountain House talk nothing but MRA. Yet, by some strange anomaly, the British registration is " The Oxford Group."

That registration was effected in 1939—the year *following* the birth of Moral Re-Armament. The explanation, doubtless, is that no one at that time—not even the omniscient Dr Buchman—could foretell the magical way in which that new phrase was destined to capture imagination in the States.

So, something of a shock awaits us when we examine the British Articles of Association, for we find that the primary aim of the Oxford Group is given as " *the advancement of the Christian religion.*"

Separate registrations followed for the United States and Canada to meet the requirements of company laws in those countries. The articles of the American incorporated body of the Group are prefaced as follows:

> Riches, reputation or rest have been for none of us the motives of association.
> Our learning has been the truth as revealed by the Holy Spirit.
> Our security has been the riches of God in Christ Jesus.
> Our unity as a world-wide family has been in the leadership of the Holy Spirit and our love for one another.
> Our joy comes in our common battle for a change of heart to restore God to leadership.
> Our aim has been the establishment of God's Kingdom here on earth in the hearts and wills of men and women everywhere, the building of a hate-free, fear-free, greed-free world.
> Our reward has been the fulfilment of God's Will.

So runs the preamble, which proves that " on paper," at any rate, the primary aim on both sides of the Atlantic is Christianity.

In practice, campaigns waged since the second world war have been of a political character. In place of " patriotism," which served well enough for a motive during the war years, the Buchmanites glibly turned to cries of " an overarching ideology," or a " supernational ideology," or an " ideology superior to Communism or any other -ism "! Or a " united ideology of Inspired Democracy."

The old talk of " winning people to Christ " has been dropped. MRA is now held out as something acceptable for people *of any race or creed.*

It is not in my power to unravel all this. I am simply stating the facts as I found them. In the bookshop at Mountain House I found a leaflet by Peter Howard entitled *The Press in an Ideological Age.* Here is an extract:

> We are living in an ideological age. This is big news. The battle is no longer only for economic and social reform, for wages and profits; it is no longer a battle for the control of territory or empire, but it is a battle to decide what ideas will capture the hearts and mobilize the wills of the masses, right across the world.

And in another leaflet by Bill Jaeger, called *How to Change a Marxist,* I found this:

> If every Marxist can change a capitalist, and every capitalist can change a Marxist, then we can change the world, and that is the programme of Moral Re-Armament.

And yet another, on *How to Change Capitalists,* by Garrett Stearly, contained this:

> How to change capitalists! Some people think it is a very difficult thing. I had supper last night with a gentleman who has been in touch with capitalists all his life. He was very sceptical about whether they could ever change. Yet it is not really very difficult. It is like elephant-hunting. You have to make a lot of preparations, but when you meet an elephant, and you know how to shoot, you can hit the target.

During my stay at Caux I amassed a great collection of leaflets and pamphlets. They were filled with the same sort of stuff. Thousands of words about " ideology "; *but not one mention of " the advancement of the Christian religion."*

But let us take a closer look at the British Memorandum and Articles of Association. I think I am right in saying that all the men responsible for controlling the Oxford Group (they are permitted to drop the " Limited " by licence from the Board of Trade) are of the Christian faith. Here are their names.

Frank N. D. Buchman, Doctor of Divinity; Roland W. Wilson, MA, Chairman and Secretary; John McC. Roots, BA; Cecil H. de V. Harvest, BScAgric.; H. Kenaston Twitchell, MA; Basil Entwistle, BA; R. M. S. Barrett, MA; A. S. Loudon Hamilton, BA; John T. Caulfeild, MA; Garth D. Lean, BA; R. O. Hicks, MA; A. Lawson Wood, MA; Raymond Nelson, MA; The Rev Julian Thornton-Duesbery, MA, Principal, Wycliffe Hall, Oxford; and Christopher Prescott.

Three of the above, Dr Buchman, John McC. Roots, and H. Kenaston Twitchell, are also on the Council of Management of the American company.

The Memorandum and Articles of Association in England open with this statement: " The Association does not claim to possess any official connection with the University of Oxford or the Oxford Society."

Conditions of association provide that no member of the Council of Management or Governing Body shall be appointed to any salaried office of the Group or any office paid by fees. Nor can they be given any remuneration except as " repayment of out-of-pocket expenses and interest . . . on money lent or reasonable and proper rent for premises . . . let to the Association."

On the other hand, all are pledged to contribute to the assets of the Association in the event of its being wound up while they are members or within one year of their ceasing to be members, for the payment of debts and liabilities.

The Council of Management is all-powerful.

Membership of the Association was given as 100 for purposes of registration, but the Council can register an increase of members should it wish to do so at any time.

It can also impose whatever conditions it chooses on

applicants for membership, such as the payment of
entrance fees, annual subscriptions, or periodical subscriptions. It can decide the terms on which a member
shall undertake work for the Group or order resignation
or cessation of membership.

*It also has powers to divide members into different classes with
different conditions of membership.*

In conducting the business of the Association, the
Council has, in fact, a free hand. One-third of its
members stand down each year, but are eligible for re-
election.

So far as Buchmanism in Britain is concerned, then, its
destinies are in the hands of the fifteen men named
above. These men are the subscribing members of the
Association, and no one else can be admitted as a member
without their sanction. And anyone who may be admitted
can be made to comply with whatever terms the fifteen
choose to devise.

Thus, we have another anomaly. From the fluid
constitution of Buchmanism, which is said to have no
actual membership, being merely an " organism," we
pass to a rigid dictatorship at the head. Any three
members of the Council of Management can form a
quorum.

How, then, does one get into Buchmanism? Remember, there is no such thing as " signing on " or taking
pledges or being sworn in or enrolled. When I asked
about this at headquarters I was told: "We are not
concerned with counting heads. What we are doing is to
get people to live an idea."

Well, for people who want to live up to the Buchmanite
standards, the first step is to be changed. " Change,
unite, fight! " is one of the favourite slogans; and Buchman himself has extended it on occasion to: " Confidence, Confession, Conviction, Conversion, Continuance."

In preceding chapters I have given a number of instances of how certain individuals became Buchmanites. A quick review shows that no two were quite the same. Loudon Hamilton, one of the first converts, was "changed," apparently, by Buchman's eloquence and magnetism; Edward Howell, the airman of Crete, was "changed" through a spiritual experience which came to him as he lay helpless in hospital; Peter Howard set out to "expose" the Group to get his name on the front page of a newspaper, but "changed" after he had tried "listening to God" as an experiment. Bernard Hallward, my fellow guest at that curious supper party in Charles Street, was drawn to Buchmanism because he saw "thirty happy people." Jack Jones, the ex-Communist I heard speak at Caux, was "changed" when his boss treated him humanly. William Yates, the Staffordshire miner, was "changed," he told me, by the ideas he heard put forward in *The Forgotten Factor*.

Reasons given for change are endless. Those simple Burmese villagers, about whom Daw Nyein Tha talked to me so eloquently over luncheon, were changed through their jealousy of other villagers who had got "that thing."

Basically, of course, it amounts to a change of heart, a desire on the part of an individual to try a new and better way of life. Most people experience such moments. When they do they are ripe candidates for Buchmanism. Perhaps they begin by offering their services. The Oxford Group gets a steady stream of free labour in this way. People offer to help. They are given unpaid work to do—office work, perhaps, typing, filing, attending to the telephone, packing, and dispatching books and pamphlets; mending linen, preparing meals.

Thus, a steady flow of recruits filters into Buchmanism. Good-hearted people who long for a chance to do something to help build a better world; old people, lonely people, frustrated people, people with too much leisure, people who just don't know what to do with themselves.

They are received with great kindness, made much of, flattered, introduced to lots of important people; made to feel important themselves. Naturally, it gratifies them to be taken notice of and to be given something to do in an organization which is obviously prosperous and flourishing and supported by celebrities galore.

One woman I met at Mountain House was delighted when they put her on sentry duty in the vestibule. " I have to see that strangers don't keep slipping in for free meals," she confided proudly. She felt truly important.

A lot of recruits feel moved to put their savings into the Group's coffers. At Caux, too, I spoke to a typist who said she had gladly given everything she possessed—a matter of £50. She was prepared, she told me, to work for the Group for nothing for the rest of her life. And she was quite confident that her economic needs would be met somehow.

When I was inspecting the Hay's Mews headquarters I was told that lots of the women I saw working happily in various departments were schoolteachers who had given up their holidays to come in and help. Of course, anyone possessing special skill or knowledge is quickly put on to the kind of work in which they can be most useful.

I asked Lean what was the routine for becoming a full-time worker, and what happened when someone came along who felt an urge to throw up a regular job in order to remake the world.

He said that before any decision could be taken the applicant's suitability for the work would have to be carefully considered by the Council of Management. If they were then satisfied that he had a true " call," he would be accepted gladly, whether he had funds of his own or not.

But, he added, newcomers were always carefully watched. No one would be put on important work without adequate training, and there would be a fairly long period of probation.

Buchmanism appeals to different people in different ways. It gives new interests to the middle-aged and elderly. It offers a form of escapism to frustrated folk; it buoys up ineffectual types who feel at a loss in the modern world.

While the rank and file are given jobs which are not too onerous, they are always made to feel that what they are doing is important. All work is done with a smile. There is a pleasant, friendly, serene atmosphere over everything. The point which strikes most visitors to Caux is this atmosphere of goodwill and cheerfulness. The Buchmanites are at peace with themselves and with life. Though they represent mixed types, they have a common bond. They feel well satisfied to be " in the swim " and to have an outlet for their energy and enthusiasm.

For the young people, of course, it can be " a lark "— plenty of good comradeship, all the fun of amateur theatricals, abundant good food, free travel, and a chance to see the world under luxurious conditions. For the older folk it is a gratifying reassurance that they are " wanted "; that there is something they can do in life; that they need never be " on the shelf."

The sexes intermingle easily and naturally at Caux. Perfect decorum is the rule. Buchmanite women use no make-up; no one smokes; no alcohol is served. All have their minds on their jobs. Dr Buchman's policy has always been to keep the women " cumbered with much serving." They enjoy it, which is why the housekeeping is maintained on such a high level.

Studying these, and other points, I came to the

conclusion that Buchmanites fall into about three classes. There is a compact inner ring of tried and trusted zealots who have been with the movement for many years, and who are almost fanatical in their beliefs. They are convinced that they have a mission in life, and they will pursue that mission to the end. It is impossible to withhold tribute for the pertinacity and consistency with which they have stood beside their leader in all circumstances. They represent the hard core of Buchmanism.

Then there is a very considerable secondary ring of ardent supporters, part-time and full-time workers, who probably came into the movement after the change-over to Moral Re-Armament in 1938. They represent all types and all classes. They are good-natured people who, without being steeped in Buchmanite lore or mysticism, work willingly for what they believe to be a good cause. Without this vast pool of unpaid labour the present ambitious activities would be impossible.

Finally, there is a vast outer ring of people who are interested enough to support Buchmanism in a lesser degree, with occasional help or financial gifts. They probably think: " It's sheer idealism, but anything is worth trying if it makes for world peace."

The control of all three rings lies in the hands of the few men at the top. In Britain, as has been shown, they number fifteen. They take all decisions; plan all campaigns; hold the purse-strings. Under their direction the men of the inner ring act as whippers-in to control the formidable secondary ring, without whose services the structure could not easily be maintained.

The whippers-in are highly-trained missionaries, well versed in psychology, able to reel off parrot-fashion all Buchman's pet slogans and arguments. They are adept in the use of flattery; adept at playing one big fish to catch another; adept at working up an emotional atmosphere

A simple, neighbourly act of kindness—the presentation of a spice cake—stops a would-be killer in The Good Road.

[*"Illustrated"*]

People of all nations unite in harmony, problems of race and creed forgotten—a spectacle which always

at Assemblies or in their stage shows. In this manner the volunteer labour pool is presumably kept filled.

* * *

With a certain intense application human strength and weakness are harnessed whenever a likely recruit presents himself. Under the heading strength I place such things as generosity, kindliness, religious fervour; under the heading weakness, snobbery, vanity, and emotion.

The façade which Buchmanism now presents to the world is undeniably impressive. But I cannot help comparing it with that of Valle Crucis Abbey, in North Wales. There it is possible for a visitor to approach from one angle and to find himself confronted by a towering edifice. He rings the bell, bolts are drawn, a small door opens—and he steps through into space! Behind that noble façade lies nothing but a tangle of long grass and a few scattered ruins.

So with Buchmanism. The façade of the World Assembly is tremendously impressive; but behind it one finds glorified YMCA meetings and juvenile amateur theatricals putting over uplift. Born in college close and cultivated on the campus, Buchmanism has never quite grown up. An aura of adolescence pervades many of its activities. One gets the impression that, for all their sincerity, the Buchmanites are playing at evangelism and dabbling in world politics.

Caux is held up as a microcosm of what life could be if everyone changed. But it seems to me fallacious. Carried to a logical conclusion the system would be unworkable. If everyone threw up his normal occupation, feeling an urge to live life as it is lived at Mountain House, there would be chaos.

Who, then, is to decide which citizens shall keep on working in the mines, in industry, or on the high seas?

M

In a microcosm it can be made to appear very attractive. Little to do but feast, dash about in big cars, or sit back and be entertained by choirs—except for taking a turn at washing up or some other chore. It is a bubble that glistens brightly so long as enough good-hearted and generous people are willing to finance it all.

But suppose, by some miracle, it *could* be carried to this logical conclusion, with all grades of workers agreeing to keep on at their jobs and to pool the fruits of their labours and to live on a share-and-share-alike basis. Doesn't that sound like Communism? Even if everyone agrees to call it " inspired democracy," it is hard to see where democracy comes in when there is no such thing as membership. No one belongs to anything. It is " only an organism." So no one has any choice. No one, that is, save a few men at the top.

Clever?

Too clever.

*   *   *

When I talked about the switch over to politics, they assured me at Caux that religion still forms the basis of Buchmanism; that the teachings have never wavered. The essence, I was reminded, is " God-Control." Early each morning the Buchmanites read their Bibles and then sit, pencil and note-book in hand, to " listen to God." They insist that all their day's programme at Mountain House, or wherever they may be, is planned with Divine Guidance. I was even asked to believe that those banal assemblies were planned in this way.

It is idle to speculate whether these promptings emanate from a living God, from the depths of the subconscious, from an individual's own conscience, from a latent " better self," or from a form of wishful thinking. The significant thing is that true Buchmanites believe them to be of Divine origin and act upon them resolutely. I respect their religious beliefs, though I cannot share them.

Few people, I imagine, doubt man's ability to strengthen his resolution and renew the spirit by communing with whatever God he believes in. But even a pagan who bows before an inanimate piece of wood may rise a better man, fortified by his superstition, comforted, reassured.

We have Peter Howard's word for it that he can recount no dramatic examples of " guidance." There was his own urge to settle up a long-outstanding debt, and his young son's urge to make his naughty little sister drink her milk. In the first one feels that ordinary promptings of decency should have been enough; in the second one feels that the parents could have been a trifle more strict.

I have, however, unearthed one or two dramatic stories of " guidance." They are taken from Buchmanite literature, so I cannot be accused of unfairness in quoting them. The first concerns a very gallant officer who " had many chances to try out this ' guidance ' in action." Faced with difficult decisions he " turned to God for direction." The guidance he received, it is claimed, proved to be dramatically correct. Another case concerns a naval officer who was said to have received " precise guidance " in the middle of a naval action which enabled him to win through to success.

I do not doubt the authenticity of such stories. It is not unusual for fighting men to pray. But I reject the idea that God could be guilty of partisanship! And might not enemy leaders have been equally entitled to guidance?

* * *

At this point a quick recapitulation seems desirable.

Buchmanism began as " A First-century Christian Fellowship "; changed to " The Oxford Group Movement "; became registered in Britain as " The Oxford

Group," which registration still stands. Now all its work is carried on under the banner of Moral Re-Armament.

What has happened to it, exactly? Is it suffering from delusions of grandeur engendered by its phenomenal successes in America during the war years, when it rocketed high on the strength of its " true patriotism " campaign? Or is the present phase destined to pass, as other phases have done?

The history of Buchmanism, as we have seen, is riddled with conflicting ideas. There is much in it that commands respect; much that is banal; much that borders upon the ludicrous. Yet, in spite of all these incongruous elements, the inescapable fact remains that a great many people of high intellectual attainments lend it support.

In fairness, their voices must be heard. I have mentioned elsewhere that the United States House of Representatives sent a bi-partisan committee to the World Assembly at Caux. A copy of the report made by this committee on its return to America is before me now. Here are a few extracts:

> Although this centre is located in a vacation utopia, visitors to the conference displayed no holiday spirit, but remained in constant attendance upon the sessions of the Assembly, held morning, afternoon, and night. Some 1,200 people filled every chair in the Assembly Hall at all meetings and an unusual enthusiasm marked each conference. . . .
>
> The committee noted with interest the presence of a delegation of 18 from Japan headed by former Prime Minister Katayama, who was the first elected post-war Premier of Japan and the first Christian to hold that post. We were informed this group made the 14,000 mile trip via the United States of America with the special permission of General Douglas MacArthur.

The report goes on to say that the presence of a committee of observers from the United States House of Representatives " seemed to arouse a grateful and enthusiastic reaction among all present, and I think the official notice taken of this movement will stimulate its

already genuine effort in the field of human relations."
In his next paragraph, the Chairman, the Hon Prince
H. Preston, Jr, of Georgia, speaks of the abundant
evidence that faith in God is the very bed-rock upon which
this movement rests.

But perhaps the most significant paragraph in his report
was the following:

> If this movement is to implement the Marshall Plan and
> the Atlantic Pact as Mr Robert Schuman, Foreign Minister
> of France, says it will by establishing an ideology of democracy
> resting on the premise that the individual is a person of dignity
> in God's sight, then it is a welcome force, which can be used
> constructively and well.

While I was at Caux the Chinese Minister to Switzer-
land came from Berne specially to read a message from
Dr Chen Li-fu, member of the Chinese Cabinet at
Canton.

> The tragic events which you see taking place in China today
> [the message ran] are a preview of what will surely happen in
> nation after nation all over the world unless the inspired ideology
> of Moral Re-Armament takes hold quickly and effectively.
> Let China be an example for all. Unless there is full change of
> heart even those nations which now may regard themselves as
> remote and secure will certainly follow in our footsteps.

Dr Chen Li-fu invited Dr Buchman to bring an
international force to China. Meanwhile, the MRA
industrial drama *The Forgotten Factor* had been translated
into Chinese, as had Dr Buchman's book *Remaking the
World*.

The Very Reverend Eugene Fischer, Dean of Strasbourg
Cathedral, who came to Caux just after the Strasbourg
Conference, said:

" At Strasbourg one met a part of Europe. Here one
meets the world. . . . Caux rightly reminds us that there
is more than Europe to plan for. There is the whole
world. . . . Can we not see in this movement a means
which Providence will use to bring certain Christian truths

to the masses who would not accept this message if it were brought to them in its traditional form? "

Dr Konrad Adenauer summed up his views as follows:

" When I am asked what particular significance Moral Re-Armament and its work has for Germany and what for Germany is particularly valuable in it, then I would reply essentially that Moral Re-Armament applies to all nations in the same way, but Germany happens to be a particular crisis point in the world. It is perhaps at that point that it is all the more important that the people find again a moral and spiritual foundation, in order to set something better against the oncoming wave of Communism."

Mr Nils Hagelin, Chief of the Aliens Department of the Swedish Home Office, said: " Caux is the centre of the new world order, and every statesman and politician must know and pay attention to Caux today."

H. E. Quinto Quintieri, Vice-President of the Italian Confederation of Industry, formerly Minister of Finance, as leader of an Italian delegation at Caux, said, at one Assembly I attended: " I believe that my country, Italy, is one where the spirit of Caux can have the widest possible repercussions. . . ."

It would be possible to cite scores of enthusiastic comments made by important delegates from all parts of the world as proof of the high esteem in which Buchmanism is held.

In Switzerland, itself, the movement has tremendous prestige. The President of " Fondation du Réarmement Morale " is Philippe Mottu, whose younger brother, Daniel, I have already mentioned as co-editor of the *Caux Information Service* bulletins.

Philippe Mottu, born in Geneva in 1913, studied banking and theology at the University there, but broke off those studies to travel with Dr Buchman. He spent two years in England and America with the Buchmanites, but returned to Geneva in 1939 and graduated in political science.

From 1940 to 1943 he was with the Swiss Army, becoming head of a section responsible for maintaining civilian morale in French-speaking Switzerland. This was part of a campaign by the Swiss military authorities to keep the three sections of the Swiss community united behind the Army Defence Policy. In the course of his duties, Mottu visited London, Helsinki, and Berlin.

In 1943 he left the Army to join the Foreign Office, and in the following year he was given permission to attend a World Assembly for Moral Re-Armament at Mackinac. He left the Foreign Office in 1945, and paid a further visit to Mackinac with ten of his fellow countrymen. It was what he saw at Buchman's American training centre that inspired him to launch Moral Re-Armament in Switzerland.

On Swiss National Day, 1949, Dr Raphael Cottier, Director of the Swiss Federal Transport Office and head of the Transport Committee for the Marshall Plan in Europe, said:

" Our Swiss Constitution, which opens with the words ' In the Name of Almighty God,' has been greatly inspired by the Constitution of that great sister republic, the United States. Is it any accident, or is it by some higher providence, that the great man to whose initiative this movement owes its beginning has connections with both countries? We as Swiss can be proud of the fact that the blood of the ancestors of Dr Buchman is Swiss blood."

And M. du Pasquier, a former Secretary of the Swiss Ministry of the Interior, writing in the *Gazette de Lausanne*, said:

If men change individually, everything round them can change. In fact, during the twenty-five [1] years of its existence,

---

[1] Moral Re-Armament was not launched until 1938.

Moral Re-Armament has had a world-wide influence,   One need only spend a few days at Caux to realize the strength of this healthy epidemic.

Another staunch supporter of Moral Re-Armament is Professor Theophil Spoerri, Rector of Zurich University, whose son is in the College of the Good Road.

" It is not my rôle to play the part of a prophet," he declared in the course of a lecture on ' Basic Forces in European History,' delivered at Caux.   " But I am convinced that in time to come men will speak of Frank Buchman even as we today speak of St Francis of Assisi. There have always been great men inspired by God in history. But what Frank Buchman has given us today is the truth that every ordinary person can be inspired by God. This is new in history. Think what it means for history that every single person, worker, factory owner, professor, student, woman, can receive guidance from God. This is the beginning of a new epoch. I am a historian. I have studied the new beginnings throughout history, and here is a new beginning that has never happened before."

Tributes of this calibre cannot be ignored.

*   *   *

Granted, then, that, with all its vagaries, Buchmanism makes a deep impression upon many eminent men, what of its future?   When I asked about this I was told that a No. 1 Priority is likely to be the completion of *The Good Road* film so that it can be made " a high-powered weapon for the leaders from countries all over the world."   About thirty or forty countries are said to be interested in it.

Strong task forces of trained MRA workers have visited Germany. Others may be sent to France, Italy, Japan, China, Malaya, Burma, and India. In addition, *The Forgotten Factor* is to be presented in New Zealand

and backed by a well-equipped task force which expects to visit Australia and South Africa as well.

When I asked, " What about Russia ? " the member of the Council of Management to whom I am indebted for this preview of things to come, shook his head. " Very difficult," he said.

In all present efforts the Buchmanites are beating one big drum, offering their ideology as the one sure answer to Communism. But now everything is overshadowed by the H-Bomb, and who can foretell the future? If by any chance the spread of Communism ceased, and the threat of World War III receded, the Buchmanites would be lost. Or would they? I don't think anything could ever perturb them. An invasion from Mars tomorrow would probably find them ready with a new pamphlet: *How to Change a Martian.*

CHAPTER 11

" *Where Does the Money Come From?* "

THIS is not my phrase. It is a poser which the Buchmanites themselves are fond of asking from time to time in their numerous publications. I have found it in a souvenir booklet of the Caux World Assembly; in the *Caux Information Service* bulletins; in the *New World News*. It figures in a pamphlet on *The Oxford Group* by J. P. Thornton-Duesbery and in *Innocent Men* by Peter Howard.

"Where does the money come from?" The Buchmanites alone have the answer, so their observations on the subject surely merit our consideration?

The Group's accounts are audited by a leading firm of chartered accountants; and, so far as the British registrations for The Oxford Group and The College of the Good Road Ltd. are concerned, the Companies Act of 1948 requires them to file detailed statements of income and expenditure. And, of course, those files are open to public inspection at any time.

Remembering that Buchmanism has no membership, no one of the many, many thousands who range under its banner has the slightest right to question the stewardship of those who hold the purse-strings. A lot of people may be curious, of course. That is a different matter. They see about them ample evidence that Buchmanism is prospering; and they are permitted to share in the bounty at table. But they have no voting power; no real say in anything. They are working for an " organism " not an " organization," they are told.

Here are a few official pronouncements on the subject of

finance.   My first is taken from a souvenir booklet on the Caux World Assembly, retailed at 1s.

Where does the money come from?

The money comes from all over Switzerland.   It comes from Swiss people, many of whom have felt that this was their best opportunity of showing their gratitude for having been spared the horrors of war.

They give their savings, their bank balance, their family jewels.   The money comes in because Mountain House is an investment for the future.

One girl gave her trousseau; a business man sold his house and gave the proceeds; others sold life insurance policies. They have invested their inheritance because they know that Moral Re-Armament, which brings the answer to social and international problems, offers the greatest security for them and their children.

For the statesmen, Caux has become the place where Switzerland no longer lives for herself alone.   Mountain House is a prepared instrument by means of which the leaders of many nations may find the quality of life and the ideology of which Europe stands in need.   They see in Caux the highest expression of Swiss foreign policy.

It is in this spirit that the Vaud cantonal authorities have freed Moral Re-Armament of all taxes payable on gifts and transfers of property.

A much more detailed explanation is to be found in *Caux Information Service* bulletin No. 9, dated August 11, 1949.

HOW IS CAUX FINANCED?

Caux is one of the best examples of how the economics of Moral Re-Armament work. . . . You know how large Caux is. How much have we invested here at Caux?   We have put in more than three million Swiss francs.   There is Mountain House, the Grand Hotel and the Hotel Maria which together give us over a thousand beds.

The Assembly this year will cost well over one million francs. Thousands come to Caux from countries which cannot provide them with currency but whose future is of the utmost importance to Europe.   The contribution of men and women trained at Caux to countries like Germany, France, Austria, and Italy cannot be calculated.   The ideology they take from Caux to their countries may be decisive for the future of Europe.

Caux has been made possible through the sacrificial giving

of many Swiss and many from other nations. People have given from their incomes. People have given from their capital. Some have given all they had in the world for Caux. A Bernese cook gave her life-savings and came here to work in the kitchens herself without salary. A young Swiss couple with three children gave their entire fortune. People have sold their life insurances, their houses, their possessions. . . . A friend of mine [this article is signed M. Robert Hahnloser,[1] of Zurich] put aside 10,000 francs to build a ski hut for his children. He decided that Caux could mean more for the future of his children than a ski hut, and gave the money to Moral Re-Armament. Swiss people sometimes have a stocking under their pillow, and there are pieces of gold in it. This gold has come here to pay for Caux.

The writer then goes on to say that it costs 15,000 francs a day to keep Caux going, adding: " We need the help of an ever-widening circle of people if that money is to be found."

In *Innocent Men,* first published in 1941, Peter Howard writes:

One thought stuck in my mind like a bramble in a sheep's coat, all the time that I was living with these people, liking them more and more, beginning to understand their ways, and yet still rather on guard against them. And here it is: *Where did the money come from?*

He says he watched events at Hay's Mews with immense care, trying to discover who paid the baker, the butcher, and the telephone bill. He discovered that the Buchmanites lived by faith. " The Group believe that God will provide all material resources for those who listen and obey." Howard offered to pay for his own board, only to find that one of the Buchmanites had " received guidance " to pay for him.

He states emphatically:

No public or private appeal for funds is ever made. . . . The Oxford Group are the only considerable body of people I know in the world today who put money very low in the scale of values.

---

[1] Since deceased. M. Hahnloser was himself a generous supporter of MRA.

Then he asks:

> In what kind of way does money come to the Group? . . .
> The fact is that the Oxford Group is supported, like most
> pioneer movements, by the sacrifices of those whom it has
> helped and who believe in it. . . . A labourer, now in the
> Army, sends 10s. a month to Hay's Mews. A squadron leader
> with the Bomber Command has, for months, sent half his pay.

To this he adds a story of a maid who had received
" guidance " to give up her weekly paper and to send the
threepence to the Group.

In *The World Rebuilt, the True Story of Frank Buchman
and the Men and Women of Moral Re-Armament*, published in
January 1951, Peter Howard declares:

> There have been thousands of small gifts not from surplus, but
> from sacrifice. . . . From the earliest days Frank Buchman's
> work has advanced through the sacrifices of those who believe
> in it. Men offer for the faith they hold most dear the things
> they count most precious. People have given of their wages,
> their capital, their houses, their savings.

He goes on to say that every pound in MRA goes far
farther than in any commercial concern or government
department.

> Hotels, garages, printing, medical, and dental care are often
> provided free or at a minimum cost by those of every nation who
> wish to spread this ideology around the world. . . . Every
> activity of MRA is planned to combine the greatest advance of
> the work with the most economic use of funds and services so
> sacrificially provided.

In his pamphlet *The Oxford Group*, J. P. Thornton-
Duesbery writes:

> From the first days the Group has advanced through the
> sacrificial giving of those who believe in its mission. People
> have given of their wages, their capital, their houses, their
> jewellery, their savings. The spirit of sacrifice at the heart of
> the work has elicited a like spirit from those who have heard
> the Group's message. No appeals have been made for funds.
> People have spontaneously contributed what they had—food,
> hospitality, time, talents, skill and experience—as well as
> money.

He amplifies this by listing four " main sources " of income :

1. Donations which people give as they are able from time to time.
2. Regular gifts made under covenant for a period of seven years or longer.
3. Legacies and interest on them.
4. The Group has also made use of literature [1] as a means of spreading its Christian message as widely as possible and any funds from this source are available for the general purpose of the Group's work, but, in fact, the greater part of the proceeds have been used again to extend the publications side of the work.

The writer then explains that the work done is out of all proportion to the Group's budget because so many people give their services for nothing. He also reveals that

Normal business and professional services, such as hotels, garages, printing or medical attention, have often been given free or at a minimum cost. . . . Further, otherwise heavy office and domestic expenses have been constantly lightened because large numbers of extra helpers, who may have little or no money to give, have unstintingly undertaken cleaning, dish-washing, cooking, typing and other necessary services, in addition to their own normal work.

Finally, contends this same authority, the Group is always careful to take advantage of large-scale planning to obtain favourable rates.

*   *   *

When I asked in London for more details I was handed a copy of a balance-sheet for the Oxford Group for the year ending September 30, 1947. This, I found, was the first full statement returned under the Companies Act, 1948. Before that the Group was not required to detail income and expenditure. The total income was

[1] J. P. Thornton-Duesbery's pamphlet is retailed at 1s.

given as £69,894, of which £55,513 was accounted for as follows:

Gifts under covenant	£10,105
Other gifts	20,408
Legacy	25,000

Interest from investments, less tax, was given as £362; interest on bank deposit as £21. Sale of literature had yielded £8,228; royalties had brought in £1,293; receipts from hostels £4,477. Total expenditure for the year amounted to £51,625, leaving a margin of £18,269.

Expenses of Head Office, including rent, rates, etc., were shown as £8,569. £4,885 was said to have been expended on unspecified purchases, " mainly literature." Maintenance of canteens and hostels accounted for £27,701; travel and other expenses, £7,451; professional charges of accountants and solicitors, £1,689.

Some individual items under Head Office and general expenses gave a clue to the volume of business done in the year. Telegrams, telephone calls, and cables cost £3,691; postage, £854; printing and stationery, £826; lighting, etc., £2,261; sundries, £210.

Total assets were valued at £126,088, including £72,172 for hostels and offices, £1,068 for car and lorry, £8,531 for stocks of literature, and £508 for other stocks.

Investments totalled £46,423, including £36,364 in war bonds and £5,000 in 3½ per cent War Loan.

Balance at bank and cash totalled £10,388, of which £6,224 was on deposit.

Since then, the Group has filed several statements of account. The return for the year ended March 31, 1952, shows an expenditure of £62,320 against an income of £54,757, the deficit being made up by a contribution from the General Fund.

As we have had numerous explanations of where the

money comes from, it will be interesting to cite some examples from the official return which reveal where the money goes.

Under Income and Expenditure we find the following items:

	£
Rent and rates	432
Repairs and decorations	264
Lighting, heating, and insurance and cleaning	748
Postage, telegrams, telephone, and cables	5,746
Printing and stationery	2,686
Sundries	634

Under hostels and hospitality we find:

	£
Rent and rates	2,015
Repairs and redecoration	6,091
Lighting and heating	2,855
Contributions to hospitality full-time workers	2,110
Catering supplies	7,951
Wages, cleaners	2,780
Miscellaneous household supplies	471
Laundry	411
Sundries	702

Travelling and motor expenses, the precise nature of which is not given, account for £6,487. Overseas travelling expenses, £3,429. Depreciation of cars and lorries, £1,651.

In the five and a half years since it started filing income and expenditure accounts, the Group has apparently got through a total of £332,876—an excess of £17,721 over income.

These figures, interesting though they are, relate to a comparatively small part of Buchmanite activities. For an outsider to gain a comprehensive idea of the total resources would be wellnigh impossible. Even if balance sheets relating to the Swiss, American, and

Canadian registrations could be examined, the searcher would still be very far from completing the picture.

* * *

Numerous other activities are engaged in, and it seems to be the practice of those in authority to favour a bulkhead system by which many undertakings, though vital parts of the Buchmanite programme, are separately financed.

The College of the Good Road Ltd, for example, is registered under the Companies Act 1948, each member's liability being limited to one pound. Its Memorandum and Articles of Association lists its objects as:

> To educate young men and women for service and leadership in a world needing spiritual guidance and a satisfactory ideology.
>
> To pursue the studies of history, economics, literature, art, music, philosophy, industry, and human relations in industry for their contribution to the understanding, guidance, and amelioration of life.

Like the Oxford Group, it is an Association " not for profit." All those who teach, lecture, or work with the students give their services " as a contribution towards building a new world." So far, it is claimed, the College has been financed by the sacrificial giving of students and others.

Now industrial houses, trade unions, Service Clubs, Foundations, and private individuals are being invited to help. The cost of training a student for one year is given as £600, which includes accommodation, food, and travel. So people are invited to provide scholarships of from £100 to £600 a year, or scholarships of £50 which will enable a student to attend the annual six-weeks training course at Caux.

The prospectus itself serves as another source of revenue,

N

for it is offered for sale at 6 francs in Switzerland or 6s. in England.

The first statement of accounts, filed October 16, 1952, shows that from its formation in October 1949 to September 30, 1950, the College received gifts for tuition and general purposes amounting to £7,731, and £1,000 from the Oxford Group for its prospectuses. Its members contributed £14 14s. and Associate Members contributed £294 7s. 5d.[1]   After spending £4,798 1s. 3d. on travelling, £1,486 2s. 10d. on board and lodging and other items, it ended its first year with a balance of £688 8s. 1d.   It charged no fees for students' tuition and maintenance.

*   *   *

Then there is the Westminster Memorial Trust, which controls money subscribed for the purchase of the Westminster Theatre to make it available for the showing of Moral Re-Armament plays as a living memorial to those who gave their lives in World War II.   Let it speak for itself in a statement which was issued in 1946 on behalf of the Trustees.

> The theatre was bought and vested in Trustees in order to bring before the nation the spirit that can meet the tasks of peace.
> More than a thousand people, from every section of British life, impressed with the seriousness of the present national and international situation, contributed the funds for the purchase of the theatre.
> Service men and women gave their gratuities. Miners, textile workers and other trade unionists, housewives, industrialists, business and professional men—all have had a part in this mobilization of resources to help to sustain a God-inspired democracy on the forward march.

This statement is signed by Rear-Admiral Sir Edward Cochrane, KBE, Major-General G. O. de R. Channer,

[1] A special resolution passed at a meeting at Caux on December 19, 1949, provided powers to accept any members of the teaching profession or Education Committees or any other person acceptable to the Board as " Associates."

CBE, MC, Wing-Commander Edward Howell, OBE, DFC, Ronald Chamberlain, MP, Alderman Fred Welch, Mayor of East Ham, 1944–45, and R. Stuart Sanderson, woollen manufacturer, of Galashiels.

The purchase price of the theatre was £132,500, and when not required for MRA shows the building is leased for ordinary theatrical enterprises. In actual fact very few MRA shows seem to have been produced there.

The licensee of the theatre is Mr James Kenneth Lindsay, of 44, Charles Street, who is also part proprietor of the Moral Re-Armament magazine *New World News*. There are four Trustees, and the Trust itself is recognized as a charity for taxation purposes, having been formed for the " Advancement of the Christian Religion and for no other purpose."

* * *

When *The Good Road* revue was presented in England at the Theatre Royal, Birmingham, and His Majesty's Theatre, London, this, again, was treated as a separate project, a National Committee of Invitation being formed for the occasion.

In the *New World News* for February 1949 an accountant who assisted the Hon Treasurer tells how it was done, his article bearing the now familiar heading: " Where Does the Money Come From ? "

He says that 60,000 people saw *The Good Road* on a free-admission basis.

> At the start there was nothing in the bank [he writes]. Many closely associated with the venture turned out their pockets. A clerk not only gave up every evening to help with the books, but sold his last security. Another man gave half of his small capital. But these were small sums and the total (£20,000 was the estimated need) still seemed a tremendous figure.

Though he vouches for the fact that there was no public appeal for subscriptions, money flowed in.

> Opening the morning's mail was a perpetual surprise [he
> declares]. Someone writes from the West : " We have sold our
> savings certificates and send you the money." An old lady with
> a shaky hand begs " to enclose something towards the expenses."

A naval officer sent all his war gratuity. A typist sent
the proceeds from the sale of her bicycle. Someone
sent valuable rings. Four members of the orchestra
returned part of their wages.

Accompanying this article was the facsimile of a typewritten statement including such items as :

		£	s.	d.
Machinist	...		12	6
Labour Editor	...	10	0	0
Widow	...	1	0	0
M.P.	...	2	0	0
Shop girl	...		5	0
Bus driver	...		15	0
Clerk	...		3	9
Housewife	...		7	6
Railway worker	...		3	6

The same statement included several substantial items.
£1,000 from an " Eng. Company "; £500 from an
" Exporting firm "; £250 from " Kenya farmer "; £107
from " 15 Teachers "; £194 15s. 10d. from " Officer ";
£100 from " Doctor." As seems usual in explanatory
articles of this kind, there is a reminder that money is still
needed for this and future campaigns.

* * *

Mention has already been made of literature as a source
of income. From what I have seen of the bookshops at
Mountain House, Caux, and Hay's Mews, London, it is
evident that the total revenue from this source, when
America and Canada are included, must be very substantial indeed.

A total sale of 850,000 copies is claimed for the Peter
Howard books alone,[1] and I was told in London that he

---

[1] Since this figure was named a sale of more than 500,000 copies of
The World Rebuilt has been claimed. U.S. manufacturers are said to
have donated 100 tons of paper for this and other MRA publications.

gives all royalties to the Group. The Group also benefits from the sale of *Escape to Live* by Edward Howell. Dr Buchman's *Remaking the World* has been a money-spinner, with editions in Danish, Dutch, German, Norwegian, French, Swedish, and Chinese.

Big circulations seem the rule with Oxford Group publications. *How to Read the Bible, How to Listen* by Roger Hicks, achieved a sale of 540,000 copies. Books, reports, pamphlets, and leaflets by the score are listed at all prices and in half a dozen languages. There are even books with Buchmanite themes for children.

When it is remembered that many Buchmanite propaganda books are produced on free paper, it will be realized that the profit must be far higher than is usually enjoyed in normal commercial publications.

Then there is revenue from the sale of gramophone records of Moral Re-Armament songs, from sheet-music, and from song-books. A catalogue I picked up at Mountain House, which covers these activities, runs to sixteen pages.

There is also the monthly magazine *New World News*, the annual subscription to which is 7s. 6d., the circulation being 50,000 copies. And yet another separate venture is " Positive Productions," used by the Group for conducting a picture agency and in connection with short film productions.

New World News is a business names registration which came into being at the end of 1945 to act as " publishers." " Positive Productions," registered in February 1947, is similarly the business name for two proprietors, one of whom is the Rev Alan Thornhill, who is also a Governor of the College of the Good Road. According to the official file, it was formed to act as " film producers."

There are other offshoots of Buchmanism, but the

examples given will serve to indicate the widespread nature of its subsidiary enterprises.

*   *   *

At the beginning of 1949 the parent body, The Oxford Group, figured in a legal dispute, appealing from a decision of the Special Commissioners of Inland Revenue that the movement was subject to income tax.

Its plea that, as an incorporated body existing for charitable objects only, it was exempt from tax, was rejected by Mr Justice Croom-Johnson. In delivering judgment he declared that the words " or benevolent " in a specific paragraph in the Memorandum of Association left the door wide open for anything which The Oxford Group might seek to do in connection with its activities, and a further paragraph also left the door wide open for it to do things which were not charitable in the legal sense.

In fact, the Oxford Group had, under that provision, obtained theatre tickets for people visiting this country, and who were studying the ideals of the Oxford Group. There was no language in the Memorandum of Association to indicate that the objects in those sub-paragraphs were subsidiary only.

His lordship added that he thought that the Memorandum of Association had been deliberately drawn in a wide form so that people could be caught in the wide net—he used the phrase in no offensive sense—cast by the Oxford Group with the object of making them religious-minded. But it was impossible to say that the Oxford Group had established that they were a body which had only charitable objects, and the appeal would therefore be dismissed.

The Group, not accepting this ruling, took the case to the Court of Appeal, but were again rebuffed. Lord Justice Tucker observed: The answer to the question whether or not they were a body established for charitable purposes only depended on the construction of the Memorandum of Association.

It was clear that the provision in paragraph B for the " maintenance, support, development, and assistance of the Oxford Group Movement in every way " permitted, or indeed required, social, political, or other activities which extended far beyond religious activities.

He thought the Memorandum of Association permitted the company to engage in purely secular activities.

It was, in his view, impossible to hold that the Oxford Group were established for charitable purposes only, and the appeal would therefore be dismissed.

Mr Justice Cohen agreed that paragraph B was very vague and would allow the Group to do anything they liked, and on that ground he agreed that the appeal should be dismissed. But he also thought that the purposes set out in paragraphs C (9) and (10) were not merely ancillary to the main objects of the Group, and the wording of those sub-paragraphs showed, as held by Mr Justice Croom-Johnson, that the Group were not established for charitable purposes only, and on that ground also the appeal failed.   Lord Justice Singleton agreed with his two colleagues.

Leave was given for an Appeal to the House of Lords; but when I inquired about this at the Buchmanite headquarters I was told that the Group had decided not to take the matter any farther, but intended to alter its Memorandum of Association.

It has, in fact, made various alterations to its Memorandum of Association, and a note in its official file at Bush House, dated March 31, 1952, states : " The Oxford Group has been recognized as a Charity under the Income Tax Act 1918 from April 22, 1950."

This means that it is now officially entitled to recover

Income Tax on covenanted subscriptions and on investment income.

* * *

Before leaving the subject of finance I must mention a system which appears to be fairly extensively favoured by full-time Buchmanites. There are men who, though they have thrown up their normal occupations, nevertheless appear to be living in comfort. Some have the use of mansions in Mayfair, are always well dressed, and often have smart cars at their disposal.

How, if they receive no salaries from Group funds, are they able to do it? The answer I was given is that they are " helped " by private supporters. This is explained and justified as follows: A young man receives a call to devote himself to Buchmanism to the exclusion of everything else. Some friend or sponsor, it seems, is always forthcoming and ready to send the worker gifts in cash and kind. All those I met appeared to lack nothing.

The system is recognized by those in power. It is thus always open to any full-time worker to do the best he can for himself. If he can " change " some wealthy sponsor, and if in gratitude that sponsor chooses to make him a regular allowance and present him with a motor-car to further his work, that is entirely his own affair. Some, I was told, enter into a legal arrangement with their sponsors, who covenant to support them for a number of years.

However successful they may be in this respect, they are not required to pool any cash they receive, and, of course, items like this never appear in Group accounts. The men themselves have no compunction about solving their economic problems in this fashion. To them it is the most natural thing in the world. "Where God guides, He provides," they say, justifying themselves with this familiar Buchman slogan.

Thinking this system wide open to abuse and calculated to undermine any man's moral fibre, I tackled a member of the Council of Management about it. He professed surprise that I should think it desirable that full-time workers should be required to account for any money they might collect individually from well-wishers or others. Here are his actual words:

" Personal gifts from one person to another are a private matter, and are no more subject to inquiry than private gifts to private persons anywhere." He added that it was quite true that motor-cars are given, " but it has only happened in a few cases, and in each case he car is given for an essential job for which it is needed rather than to the person for his own use and pleasure. . . .

" The real point of the personal economic system of the Group is that we aim at a system where, as Dr Buchman says, everybody cares enough and everybody shares enough and so everybody has enough. This means that on the personal side we would not, of course, attempt to control or know about all the gifts from one individual to another."

So, you see, the " personal economic " system is firmly established and fully recognized in Group circles as " the done thing."

On the other hand, the Group argues that it is cheaper for a number of its full-time workers to share one house than to maintain separate establishments, and that some of them have private means which they pool for the common good. I gladly give this explanation.

*　　*　　*

To sum up on finance, it will have been noted that three spokesmen who have been cited in this chapter have stated categorically that no public appeal for funds is ever made. A verbal assurance to the same effect was also given to me personally during one of my interviews with leading Buchmanites in London. Yet readers can hardly have failed to observe that some of those articles explaining where the money comes from also embodied appeals for fresh funds! I, myself, heard an appeal for 3,000,000 Swiss francs launched from the platform at Mountain House during one Assembly; and other appeals have been launched since.

For over thirty years the Buchmanites have been liberally supported with money—money to spread the Christian religion, money to " remake " the world, money to foster patriotism, money to buy hotels, money to buy a theatre, money to finance stage productions, money to finance a film, money to finance a College, money to combat Communism.

This last-named object is being held up as an insurance for the future and for generations yet unborn. At the close of the 1949 World Assembly at Caux an appeal was launched from the platform in the following terms:

" Many individuals have given. They have given all their possessions, all their capital. And people all over the world have begun to help. I think of the Italians who were here today. I think of the Finns who were not able to send money but sent us chairs. I think of all the countries whose currency is weak, and where, in spite of that, people have fought to see that their countries also took part in the cost of Caux.

" The Conference of Caux has been larger this year, and it will cost more than the normal one million Swiss francs. We have our film of *The Good Road* which will go as a weapon to every part of the world. And we have all the task forces which must go out from here throughout the world.

" So I believe that today must be for each one of us a day of decision. A decision as to what our contribution is to be. What is my part in the building of this new world? But there is a greater question—not only concerned with my own part. What shall be the part of my country? Because this is the greatest revolution of all time, this revolution in which we are living, every land can and wants to take part in it. I have just received a telegram from one small country in Europe. It promises us one hundred thousand Swiss francs. We need to take time now to decide, each for himself, where is my part in the advance? What part can my country play? "

Thus the begging is lifted at once on to an international plane. All countries are invited to contribute, and if they can't send cash, then goods will do. And the bogy now being flourished with effect is Communism. " Pay up! Or the Communists will get you! " is the virtual war-cry.

Mention has been made in another chapter of the fact that visitors to Caux who may have no Swiss currency to spare are told that they may, if they wish, contribute in their own country after they return home. Names and addresses of collectors are supplied to make it easy for them. So far as the United Kingdom is concerned, an address is given in Kensington which proves, on inquiry, to be that of a private residential flat. It is puzzling to know why intending contributors could not be asked to send their offerings to Moral Re-Armament's London headquarters direct.

For over thirty years, I repeat, well-meaning people have poured money into the Buchmanites' coffers. Immense sums must have passed through the Group's hands—and more and more money is needed as the Movement grows. Yet, as I have shown, not even the most earnest supporters have any say in how the money is spent. That rests with a handful of men at the top. They are men of high ideals and strict integrity, but they are the virtual Dictators of Buchmanism—as powerful relatively as the men in the Kremlin.

But let us turn from this materialism. " People are more important than things." Before we say farewell to Buchmanism, let us take a look at the man who started it all.

CHAPTER 12

The Man Who Started It All

In a materialistic sense Dr Frank Nathan Daniel Buchman is undoubtedly the most successful evangelist of his age; in a spiritual sense his gains are less easy to calculate. He is " Frank " to unspecified thousands of followers, but he has always insisted that he is not concerned with counting heads but with diffusing an idea. That he has done throughout the past thirty years of his life with a persistence all can respect, and with a flair for publicity which many a commercial firm might envy.

I have not left him till last from any feeling of disrespect. His rôle is far too important for that. He is the bridge-builder, and he holds in his hands a number of key pieces which will complete the jig-saw picture I have been trying to piece together.

As " the proper study of mankind is man," so the proper study of Buchmanism is Buchman. Indeed, it is impossible to understand that fantastic growth without considering the life-story of the man who planted the simple seed from which it sprang. There is nothing very remarkable in Buchman's background, but here and there a sudden flash illumines some of the dark corners of Buchmanism far more effectively than any Group apologist has done.

Frank Buchman is not the complex character some have sought to make him. Nor is there anything saintly about him, though admirers have likened him to St Francis of Assisi. Nor can I agree with those who see him as a mystic. He is a bachelor, he confides, because he was never " guided " to marry.

I think the best characterization I have seen comes from Alan Thornhill, a disciple of many years' standing whose early morning lecture I attended on my last day at Caux. It occurs in an introduction to *Remaking the World*, and runs: "No man would more readily admit that he is fallible, that he like other men can miss the way. He would claim nothing for himself that is not available to everyone."

In other words, an ordinary man. By what means, then, has this ordinary man risen to his present eminence?

At forty-three he was a wandering missionary with an unimpressive background; at seventy-five he heads what has been described as "the most successful movement since Christian Science." Few would deny him credit for tenacity of purpose and a gift for inspiring others with a zeal often more fanatical than his own.

Buchman spent his boyhood in Pennsburg, Pennsylvania, where he was born on June 4, 1878. One hundred and thirty-eight years before, the sailing-ship *Phoenix* had brought his Swiss ancestors to the New World. They were from St Gallen.

He seems to have been a normal youngster, fond of fishing and swimming. Quite early he displayed a facility for making friends. At the risk of disrupting household economy he would invite everyone he met to dinner.

He graduated at Muhlenberg College and, as an ordained Lutheran minister, went to work in what was then the poorest part of Philadelphia. After three years with his church he left to found the first Lutheran hospice and settlement house for poor boys. As a student he had been shy and reserved, but the work he had chosen toughened him sufficiently to force him into a dispute with the trustees of the hospice. The young pastor protested that his flock were not being sufficiently well fed, and when no notice was taken of his protests he promptly resigned.

That, according to some accounts, was in 1908, and, hearing of a religious convention that was being held at Keswick, he seized the opportunity to visit England. He was thirty, and perhaps he thought he could escape from his troubles by putting the Atlantic between himself and the older men with whom he had quarrelled.

But his conscience troubled him. Was he right to nurse resentment against those trustees? He began to reproach himself for bearing ill will; he told himself that he was proud and selfish. He may have felt sorry, too, for the poor boys he had left behind. In this miserable frame of mind he wandered into a little village church in Cumberland, where, while listening to a woman preacher, he suddenly beheld a vision of the Cross.

His sense of oppression and uncertainty left him. He was a " changed " man. One of his first acts was to write to the trustees of that poor boys' hostel in America offering his humble apologies. They never troubled to reply. So that chapter of his life was closed.

* * *

Buchman next secured a post as YMCA secretary in the State University in his native Pennsylvania. How long he remained in that post is uncertain. Most accounts I have read agree that he went to the university in 1909, but no one seems to know when he left it.

According to one prominent Buchmanite, John McCook Roots, he left in 1915 to tour for a year in India, Korea, and Japan with Sherwood Eddy, then YMCA secretary for Asia. But *Who's Who in America* gives the date of that tour, under Eddy's biography, as 1911. Buchman's biography, in the same volume, states that he spent the war years looking after prisoners. Roots makes no mention of this, but says Buchman returned to America in 1916 as extension lecturer at Hartford Theological Seminary.

In *Drawing-Room Conversion,* published in 1950, Dr Allan W. Eister mentions that Dr Buchman was requested to leave the campus after students had complained that his activities interrupted their studies. At any rate he was in the Far East again from 1917 to 1919. Alan Thornhill's biographical sketch in *Remaking the World* skips this period altogether and leaps from 1909 to 1921.

Our own *Who's Who* and *Who's Who in America* both omit all reference to Buchman's work with the poor boys' hostel. Instead they say that in 1908 he was travelling in the Near East, including Turkey, Greece, and Egypt.

A Buchmanite pamphlet called *An Approach to Remaking the World* states that Buchman formulated his theory of life-changing while crossing the Pacific in 1917, and adds: " During much of this time Frank Buchman was in China and India as well as USA." From this same source I gather that this was a formative year in which Buchman was experimenting in life-ch ... quiet times, house-parties, and assemblies.

In the summer of 1918, at Kuling, a resort in Central China, Buchman staged his first real house-party. He gathered together a group of about a hundred Chinese and foreign Christians—a mixed bag of pastors, missionaries, statesmen, business, and professional men. The party went on for a couple of weeks.

Buchman was still in China in 1919, for it was there that he met two Anglican Bishops who, learning that he proposed to revisit England, asked him to look up their sons at Cambridge. Again I have found discrepancy in Buchmanite chronicles of what happened next. McCook Roots says he looked up the Bishops' sons and took them with him to America in 1920. Thornton-Duesbery says: " He went to Cambridge in 1920, and from there came to Oxford in 1921."

Alan Thornhill, on the other hand, writes:

> In 1921 Frank Buchman was invited to Washington by a
> military member of the British delegation to meet delegates to
> the Disarmament Conference. Hopes were high that Pacts
> and Leagues would outlaw war. He was convinced that nothing
> would succeed unless the transforming power which he had seen
> at work in individuals be brought to nations. As he travelled
> on the night train to Washington, the conviction came to him to
> resign the comfortable University post which he held.

He evidently met with some set-backs in 1926 when he
presided over The Philadelphian Society at Princeton
University. After an official inquiry Dr Buchman was
barred from the Campus by President Hibben. His
methods were described as " dangerous from medical and
psychological viewpoints." This phase is dealt with in
some detail in Dr Eister's book.

*   *   *

One thing, however, can be clearly established. In the
first forty-three years of his life Frank Buchman had
achieved nothing of any consequence. He had dabbled in
slumming; dabbled in YMCA work; held a brief post
as theological lecturer; and had dabbled in missionary
work and experimental evangelism. How was it, then,
that this very ordinary man, with such an unpromising
background, came to make such a forceful impact upon
Oxford ?

I have given Loudon Hamilton's personal testimony of
the astonishing impression this middle-aged American
made upon the members of the Beer and Beefsteak
Society, and how students would queue for hours just to
secure a short interview with Buchman. Hamilton's
enthusiasm as he told me these things was as fresh as if
they had happened the night before.

In those early Oxford days, of course, there was not the
slightest inkling that Buchmanism would ever develop

o

into a world movement. Buchman himself was chiefly absorbed in personal evangelism, the saving of individual souls by his own mixture of psycho-analysis and religion. " Soul-surgery " is how the late Harold Begbie described it in his book *Life Changers*.

There is no doubt that Buchman worked with terrific application. Sometimes he would be closeted for hours with one man, delving into case-history, exploring inner recesses of the mind, acting as father confessor. Most of his subjects, it would seem from Begbie's account, were troubled by what Benjamin Franklin termed " that hard-to-be-governed passion of youth."

Says Begbie:

> The University shepherds altogether ignored this suffering of their flocks. No doctor ever lectured on the subject, no moralist offered a word of advice. The young men were left to fight the matter out among themselves, chiefly in secret.

He cites many examples of " cases " helped by Buchman. One young soldier went to see Buchman alone just before ten o'clock and did not leave until past two in the morning. Begbie met him next day, " his pale face and suffering eyes lighted by a strange smile of boyish gladness and triumphant serenity, in spite of all the marks of a sleepless night and great spiritual strain which showed behind the brightness of his face like so many bruises." I saw a few young people with faces like that at Caux.

As a practised YMCA secretary and with the experience of his missionary work behind him, it cannot have been very difficult for Buchman to size up the individual needs of the adolescents who sought his advice.

Interviewed by Begbie he said that he considered privacy essential to his method ; that he regarded publicity as a grave danger.

> His genius, I think [Begbie wrote] lies in thinking with an intense preoccupation of individual persons. . . . Any idea of " mass production " in his work is to him dreadfully repellent.

Therefore it is that he shuns publicity of any kind, and never for one moment dreams of calculating his gains in statistics.

Begbie gives him credit for having " changed " the very life of a student in the course of conversation—" as profoundly and persuasively as ever I have known it changed by devoted missionaries among the ignorant and base."

It is interesting, I think, to give this independent author's description of Buchman's physical appearance at that time.

> In appearance he is a young-looking man of middle life, ll, upright, stoutish, clean shaven, spectacled, with that mien f scrupulous, shampooed, and almost medical cleanness, or fresh ness, which is so characteristic of the hygienic American.
> His carriage and his gestures are distinguished by an invariable alertness. He never droops, never slouches. . . . Few men so quiet and restrained exhale a spirit of such contagious well-being. . . . I am tempted to think that if Mr Pickwick had given birth to a son, and that son had emigrated in boyhood to America, he would have been not unlike this amiable and friendly surgeon of souls.

Somehow, I don't think the quiet phase of personal evangelism at Oxford lasted very long. Later commentators among the Buchmanites say that Buchman's real purpose in concentrating upon the university students was " to create leadership " for plans he already entertained for giving his ideas world scope. This sounds reasonable, and it ties up with my theory that he drew some of his inspiration from Confucius.

Confucius held that moral order must precede political order. So does Buchman. Confucius loved good food. So does Buchman. Confucius trained 3,000 young followers. Buchman has trained " a lot of little Wesleys." Confucius taught: " If we could all be courteous for even a single day the hatreds of humanity would turn to love."

Buchman has taught his followers to sing: *Sorry is a Magic Little Word.*

*   *   *

Almost from the first, Buchman's personal evangelism was supplemented by " house-parties," held in country homes or at hotels. They seem to have been Caux gatherings in miniature, minus the theme songs and showmanship, and confined to an exchange of personal religious problems rather than talk of ideology or world problems.

There is no record that I have been able to discover to show at what stage financial support was sought for A First-century Christian Fellowship, which was what Buchmanism passed as at that time. It must have been necessary to raise money at a fairly early stage, for Buchman soon started travelling backwards and forwards across the Atlantic with growing parties of smartly dressed young followers.

His policy of cultivating " the best people " was undoubtedly useful when the need for funds made itself felt, though when asked why he always went after wealthy and influential people his stock reply was that they helped to bring in others. That policy still holds good and is the subject of frequent comment.

The early house-parties attracted varying numbers, from twenty to 150. Sometimes they were week-end affairs; sometimes they were prolonged for ten days. Young people in the twenties predominated. It was the practice, I believe, for them to contribute 5s. a head as " registration fee."

The purpose of house-parties, it was stated, was to " relate modern individuals to Jesus Christ in terms which they understand and in an environment which they find congenial." There were " informal talks on sin," and a feature of those days, apparently, was separate groups for men and women for the discussion of sex problems " in a more intimate vein than is possible in a mixed gathering."

Group historians, I note, usually skip this period, or rush through it in general terms, such as " from 1921 to 1928 Dr Buchman devoted himself to raising and training leadership in Oxford and other universities in Britain and America." They also omit to mention that in May 1928 the Oxford undergraduate paper *Isis* carried an editorial demanding that " student leaders of the semi-religious cult known as ' Buchmanism ' be suspended from the University." Buchman's own book of selected speeches, *Remaking the World*, begins with a short address delivered at Oxford in 1934 when his movement was already thirteen years old.

At some stage in those preliminary thirteen years he must have discovered that he had a formula for success. He certainly raised sufficient funds to finance trips to Holland and South Africa, a coast-to-coast campaign through Canada, and large-scale gatherings in England.

From then on he never stopped travelling. Canada, Ireland, and Norway in 1934; Norway again in 1935, and Denmark, Switzerland, and America. In 1936 he not only visited Denmark and America, but also staged a World Assembly at Birmingham which drew 25,000 people. In the following year he addressed 100,000 people at a Whitsun meeting in Utrecht, Holland, and could claim that the Group's work had spread to some fifty countries.

This four-year phase of almost non-top travel confirms that he was already flourishing. His London headquarters at that time were at Brown's Hotel, Dover Street, from which he and a close ring of associates conducted Group business.

The mystery of where all the money came from was even then beginning to excite curiosity. Asked why he didn't silence criticism by publishing accounts, Buchman replied : " Why, who would be interested in *our* accounts !

Landladies' bills and all that. We take no collections, you know. We never ask for money." Pressed as to why he and his followers always travelled in luxury and invariably stayed at the very best hotels, his equally non-committal reply was: "Why not? Isn't God a millionaire?"

Such answers typify the self-assurance success had given him. How different from the quiet newcomer to Oxford who had told inquirers thirteen years before that he considered privacy essential to his method, and who had insisted that only his initials must be used if any reference were made to his work.

From every point of view his organization was absolutely sound. He had announced lofty aims which had been fully endorsed by many Church dignitaries. No one could question those aims without immediately becoming self-branded as being in favour of dishonesty, immorality, selfishness, and hate.

His financial system was equally sound. He had created a movement that had no constitution. Frankly he could explain, beaming through his spectacles, that you couldn't join, there were no membership lists, no rules, no badges. It was just a way of life. Either you lived the Group way, or you didn't. It was all so very attractive and, of course, unanswerable.

Buchman's public addresses of those times are not impressive, read in cold print. Religion was the keynote, and some passages sound like the stump oratory of a third-rate evangelist. Yet here and there are glimmerings of what is yet to come, in phrases like: "God-controlled supernationalism is the only sure foundation for world peace," and "What we need is a supernational network of live wires across the world. . . ." "God-Control" was his key phrase at that time as "Moral Re-Armament" is today.

In 1936, America's election year, he broadcast from Philadelphia:

> Have you ever thought where America's real safety lies? America's safety lies in God-control. God-controlled individuals, God-controlled homes, God-controlled schools, God-controlled industry, God-controlled politics, God-controlled nations. . . . God is the person that the American voter has got to reckon with in the coming election. The real question is, " Will God control America. . . ."

Between 1934 and 1937, too, Buchman coined many of the slogans which his followers repeat parrot-fashion today. "When man listens, God speaks. When man obeys, God acts." " If you want the world to get straight, get straight yourself." " Everybody wants to see the other fellow changed. Every nation wants to see the other nation changed. But everybody is waiting for the other fellow to begin." " The Oxford Group believes that the ordinary person can do the extraordinary thing if he is in touch with God." " God spoke to the prophets of old. He may speak to you. God speaks to those who listen. God acts through those who obey." " Why not a spiritual radiophone in every home? "

Someone had also discovered the possibilities of Group literature as an additional source of income. In 1937 was published *Rising Tide,* a pictorial review of the Oxford Group which ran into nine editions and was translated into eight languages. A total sale of 1,500,000 copies was claimed. Thus, the four-year phase ended on a high note.

*   *   *

In an earlier chapter I have given some account of the birth of Moral Re-Armament in 1938, and I have explained how it marked a turning point in Group history. It is particularly interesting to note that Buchman's speeches from that time onward show a marked improvement in quality. He lapses far less frequently into his old

gospel-meeting jargon, and rises on occasion to considerable heights. There is a much stronger note of authority
underlying his utterances, and again and again he shows
vision and a real grasp of world affairs.

At Visby, Sweden, in August 1938, he told his hearers:
" I am tremendously interested in . . . how to save a
crumbling civilization. That is the thing that interests
me. . . . I want to reach the millions of the world."

And at Interlaken, a month later, he said:

" The Oxford Group's aim ever since the last war has
been to give a whole new pattern for statesmanship and a
whole new level of responsible thinking—faculties only
given to men who are living under God's guidance. . . .
We have set ourselves the difficult task of trying to
liquidate the cost of bitterness and fear, which mounts
daily. The odds are seemingly against us, but just as
individuals are delivered from their prison cells of doubt
and defeat, so it is possible for nations to be delivered
from their prison cells of fear, resentment, jealousy, and
depression, and oftentimes through one illumined man,
one masterful prophet. How often this has been true in
history! If this is true of one man, what can happen if a
group of people in every nation carry through the illumi-
nation and give a whole new public opinion? "

The quiet personal evangelist has burgeoned into a
forceful spiritual leader. A few days later he insisted:
" Spiritual power is still the greatest force in the world."

His speeches became longer; his periods more impressive. Broadcasting in November 1938, he said:

> We have been so long on the low levels of religious experience
> that we cannot readily grasp what an Alpine range of experience
> could be ours if all our thinking, acting, and planning were God-
> controlled and not man-controlled. We need a whole new
> creative force let loose in the world—a religious experience so
> dynamic, so wholly adequate that, in the words of Isaiah,
> " Nations shall run unto thee because of the Lord thy God."
> President Roosevelt has said: " I doubt if there is any problem

—social, political, or economic—that will not melt before the fire of spiritual awakening."

Today we drift with the tide instead of creating the experience that will turn the tide. In the recent crisis many people again turned to God. Man's extremity may be God's opportunity. But as an Edinburgh landlady told me, " It is one thing to pray during the crisis, as hundreds have done. It is another thing so to live that it does not happen again."

It was Buchman's sixtieth year—and one of his busiest. After launching Moral Re-Armament at East Ham in May, he spoke in Visby, Interlaken, Geneva, and London. And in the spring of 1939 he departed for America, to launch Moral Re-Armament there.

* * *

As Buchman set off in quest of new triumphs, the Oxford Group was encountering some minor difficulties in London. A case came before the courts in March in which the Group's claim to a legacy of £500 was contested on the grounds that, as it consisted of an indefinite and unascertainable number of persons, possessing no officers, it could not very well inherit anything.

Mr Justice Bennett, who heard the case,[1] said that affidavits had been filed in which it had been sought to show that there *was* a society having the name Oxford Group; but the evidence failed to establish the existence of any such body.

Mr Justice Bennett also commented that it seemed rather strange that there should be nobody in the group answerable for expenditure. Some accounts were mentioned covering an item of over £400 for Coronation seats, but the Group's answer to this was that the money had been donated for that especial purpose. The Judge ruled that before the Court could find that there was an association there must be some rules, written or oral, by which those supposed to be members were tied together. There must be some constitution.

[1] *The Times*, February 2, 1939 and March 10, 1939.

Through not being properly registered the Group lost its legacy of £500, a set-back which may possibly have hastened the registration of the Oxford Group, which took place five months later.

And what was Buchman doing while these important matters were being thrashed out in London? War was now imminent, and his bid of the preceding year to set himself up as a world spiritual leader with the key to peace could not be repeated. In any case, the ordinary public had not taken him very seriously—how could they when they remembered his luxury trips to and fro with droves of smartly dressed young sybarites?

While the Oxford Group was being registered with the prime object of " the advancement of the Christian religion," its irrepressible leader was making advances (perfectly proper, of course) to a world-famous star in far-away Hollywood. Believe it or not, he felt " guided " to obey Mae West's genial invitation to " come up and see me sometime." [1]

When Dr Buchman called at her Hollywood apartment she received him in a pink negligée, and a contemporary news report gives the following account of their conversation:

> *Miss West :* " You are doir ~ wonderful work."
> *Buchman :* " You are splendid character."
> *Miss West :* " I owe my success to the fact that I have been practising your philosophy in recent years."
> *Buchman :* " You've done wonderful work, too, Miss West, in pleasing and entertaining millions with your charming personality."

Happily for posterity, the pair posed together and a delightful picture was provided for the photographers showing Dr Buchman handing the dazzling Mae a slim volume on Moral Re-Armament. Of course, Hollywood loved it. With his acutely developed sense of publicity, he has

[1] *Daily Express*, August 19, 1939.

ever been ready to play to the gallery. He never objects to posing for a picture if it will give point to a campaign. He will don Burmese costume to receive a distinguished Eastern visitor, or permit Indian delegates to festoon his shoulders with traditional garlands. In Canada he appeared in full Redskin regalia as " Chief Big Light." Yet he is the man of whom Harold Begbie wrote: " He considers privacy essential . . . he regards publicity as a grave danger."

His flair for showmanship has sometimes puzzled the public. But there is method in his madness. Some antics may savour of the hot-gospeller; but Buchman understands the masses. He knows that he could not get his message to a tithe of the people by orthodox methods; but 30,000 crowded the Hollywood Bowl ɔ see the man who had " changed " Mae West.

He worked with tremendous drive and vigour throughout the war years in America, touring the country with a trained international force of 130 workers, visiting New York, Los Angeles, Washington, Georgia, Monterey, San Francisco, Philadelphia, and Mackinac Island. His meetings were lavishly organized to give the American public the spectacles he knew they loved. The four pylons of Moral Re-Armament, symbolizing the four absolute moral standards, would be raised among the flags of all nations. And a band of kilted pipers, which travelled with him, always won a great ovation.

Patriotism, national unity, and defence were his key themes on which he hung his speeches and broadcasts; but all the time he was looking ahead and paving the way for the post-war period with phrases like: " Our instant need is for millions to plan for the new world," or " America must discover her rightful ideology."

Though his American campaign was mostly unbroken triumph, there was one slight reverse. The Group were asked to cease using their national headquarters which then formed part of the Calvary Episcopal Church in New York. The request was all the more shattering because it came from the Rev Samuel Shoemaker, one of Buchman's earliest American adherents.

"When the Oxford Group was, on its own definition, a movement of vital personal religion, working within the churches to make the principles of the New Testament practical as a working force today we fully identified ourselves with it," declared the Rev Shoemaker. "Certain policies and points of view, however, have arisen in the development of Moral Re-Armament about which we have had increasing misgivings."

But America is a big place, and Buchman, travelling all the time, was probably not unduly troubled by this slight rift. He scored successes everywhere he went, and on the eve of his departure after seven prosperous years, he said: "We are in a global work. MRA is the one hope of the world."

His return to Berkeley Square headquarters in 1946 was attended by great ceremony. Hundreds of his followers lined the broad staircase, and as Buchman stood clasping a bouquet, the choir sang a lusty welcome song specially written for the occasion. "Greetings from England, Wales, Scotland, and Ireland . . ." they sang. "There is nothing we cannot accomplish . . . mighty things we shall do." Their leader rewarded them with a dignified, "Thank you. So nice to be home; so many smiling faces."

Later he told the Press: "Inspired democracy is what we want to teach, and I have come to Britain to take part in our great campaign. I believe there are three ideologies in the world today—Marxist, Fascist, and Moral Re-Armament. MRA brings a new ideology for the democracies of the world."

Asked about Germany, he replied that he had no plans for Germany. The time was not ripe. Yet, in the event, the first post-war Buchmanite advance was made in Germany in 1948, to be followed by a second big campaign in 1950.

The Buchmanites have certainly done their best to live up to their boast " mighty things we shall do." Each year they have staged bigger and better World Assemblies at Mountain House. In a world broadcast from Caux in 1947 Dr Buchman said:

> At Caux, in the heart of troubled Europe, and at Mackinac Island in America, there are centres for ideological training to which the ordinary man and the statesmen are coming in growing numbers, and they are finding there new hopes and the way out of confusion.

There is no doubt that in a few years he has put Caux on the world political map. It is on the cards that his international assemblies will grow in grandeur each year. Yet he has nothing new to offer. With infinite patience and persistence and ingenuity he rings the changes on one simple theme—that if everyone would agree to behave decently all troubles, domestic, industrial, national, and international, would melt away. Change yourself and then start changing others; and in an unspecified number of years, presumably, the world will be peopled by perfect beings.

That is Buchmanism, stripped of its jargon and superb showmanship and minus its feasting and choir and theme songs. Yet it would be unfair to Buchman to dismiss it so lightly. His genius lies in the unflagging way in which he keeps re-selling his simple ideology, bestowing upon it fresh furbishings to meet any given situation.

Consider what he has achieved. Starting when past middle age with nothing but his own burning convictions, he has created a movement which, for all its nebulous qualities, grows in influence year by year.

He has come a long way since he left those underfed boys behind in that hostel in Philadelphia over forty years ago.   I wonder what happened to them?

*   *   *

Buchman's final touch of genius lies in the way in which he has organized the Movement's finances. Wealth can flow into Group coffers from all over the world, yet no one can question the stewardship. Even with the many amendments to the Memorandum and Articles of Association of the Oxford Group, the powers wielded through that body are still astonishingly wide.

Whenever it is felt that the powers of the parent body are not elastic enough it has only to launch some fresh registration—as in the case of The College of the Good Road Ltd, or the photographic agency known as Positive Productions. That process can go on for ever, and every fresh enterprise can be financed from gifts specifically earmarked.

So though it is true to say that the registered object of the Oxford Group is " the advancement of the Christian religion," it can indulge in a limitless variety of enterprises—all financed by gifts from an ever-widening circle of supporters.

No one can challenge it, though if pressed it can always fall back on the excuse that it was " guided " to take a certain course of action. What happens when different members receive conflicting " guidance "? Suppose one's guidance reads " buy a theatre " and another's reads " buy an hotel "? Someone thought out the answer to that one long ago.

A system has been devised whereby individual guidance can be " checked " by collective guidance, with ultimate reference, if necessary, to Buchman as head of the inner ring. The " checking " is theoretically a safeguard against the inclusion of items which might only be promptings of the subconscious; but one effect is to enable a tight rein to be kept on everything.

This raises the interesting speculation of who will succeed Dr Buchman? There is no hierarchy; but possible names have been mentioned in the Press at times. There are many of Buchman's " Little Wesleys " from whom to choose, and some have gained considerable eminence in Group affairs. Alan Thornhill, Loudon Hamilton, Garth Lean, Peter Howard, are all in the running. And a person to be watched is Dr Morris Martin, a man of parts who combines spiritual qualities with business acumen. He has been Buchman's personal assistant for years, and probably knows more of the leader's inner thoughts and methods than anyone. Then there is the chairman and secretary of the Oxford Group, Roland Wilson, who has also worked closely with Buchman for many years.

Another possible candidate is Philippe Mottu, President of the Fondation du Réarmement Morale in Switzerland. Though a comparative newcomer, he has travelled widely with Buchman, and the very fact that Mountain House is now recognized as a world centre seems to favour his chances.

But Buchman may upset all calculations by making his own nomination. It is likely that he has long ago settled the problem in his own mind and has made his own preparations for a successor. At seventy-five, though, he seems as alert and shrewd as ever. His followers revere him, rush to do his slightest bidding, and quote his most commonplace utterances as if they were fraught with inspired meaning. He lets them have their head in this, though sometimes, I think, they do him disservice in their excessive adulation.

He is honoured and respected far outside his own circles.

Universities have bestowed degrees upon him, civic banquets have been given in his honour, and at the close of 1949 he was made Commander of the Royal Order of King George I of Greece.

France's former President, M. Auriol, invested him with the Knighthood of the Legion of Honour, sending Senator Eugenie Eboué to Germany to perform the investiture on his behalf.

It has been rumoured that Robert Schuman, at the time French Foreign Minister, secured this honour for him; and *The New Statesman and Nation* and other papers have hinted that if Buchman was not actually behind the Schuman Plan, then he at least helped to crea. 'he atmosphere in which it was evolved.

Buchman and Schuman have long been friends, and the French statesman has paid a visit to Caux.

Thus Buchman's power and influence continue to spread, with new campaigns also developing in Australia, New Zealand, India, and Africa.

Did the Frank Buchman of 1921, who burned midnight oil at Oxford while troubled young students bared their souls to him, dream that he would one day reach such eminence and preside over international gatherings of 24,000 delegates from eighty-eight countries?

I doubt it. It is a wise prophet who can foresee where his own predictions will lead him.

Epilogue

In presenting my picture of Buchmanism I have striven to make it three-dimensional. First, I have set forth the facts as they unfolded themselves before me in the course of a prolonged probe. These have been given without embellishment and without distortion.

Secondly, I have faithfully recorded the changing impressions those facts made upon me. I have told of things which puzzled or displeased me, but I have never withheld credit when I thought it was due.

Finally, in the interest of absolute fairness, I have quoted freely from Buchmanite literature, so that the reader could have the benefit of their authoritative explanations to offset any of my own impressions.

*   *   *

A recurrent problem has been to find ways of describing Dr Buchman's followers. I have used " Buchmanite " chiefly for consistency because it is a comprehensive term and may denote quite legitimately those of the inner ring or the much wider circle of general supporters. I am aware that the term has been used derisively in the Press at times, but I have not used it in any such sense. Besides, I can think of no better alternative.

" Grouper " has an ugly ring, and becomes less apt as the Oxford Group recedes into the background and Moral Re-Armament takes the stage. And to talk of " Moral Re-Armers " or " Moral Re-Armourers " sounds a little facetious. " Members " is inexact because there are no members—so " Buchmanites " it has to be. True followers of Dr Buchman should surely be proud of the term?

I did not embark upon this inquiry to prove or disprove anything. I was not concerned with formulating anything in the nature of an indictment; nor had I any idea of attempting to " whitewash " Buchmanism. The movement has had its traducers, but, as I have shown, it has never lacked apologists.

My probe was conducted partly for my own satisfaction. I was curious to know what lay behind the scenes. I wanted to obtain a clear, well-balanced picture of Buchmanism. But I felt also that the subject was sufficiently big and important to interest a wide public. I believed that a lot of people who had no opportunity of probing for themselves would, nevertheless, be glad to have before them enough reliable data to enable them to form their own judgment.

" That's all very fine," some people may say, " but where do *you* stand? What sort of conclusions have you reached about it all? Aren't you going to tell us? "

Frankly, I cannot see that my own opinions are of any great moment. I have performed my task of finding the facts and laying them before you. But some friends have pointed out that failure to make clear my own feelings is likely to leave me open to suspicion of trying to run with the hare and hunt with the hounds.

My friends appreciate that impartiality was desirable in presenting the facts, but they add that I can hardly remain neutral at the end. They insist that I owe it to my readers to tell them exactly what I think. So, for what they may be worth, I give my own opinions in this Epilogue. I ask no one to accept them. They represent nothing but my personal views.

* * *

First let me say that Buchmanism is something which no one can dismiss lightly. It is based, as my book shows, on Christian precepts, and its avowed aim is to foster peace on earth and goodwill toward all men. I don't think anyone can quarrel with its principles.

These crystallize the wisdom of the Ten Commandments and the Sermon on the Mount. They give expression to sentiments most thoughtful people entertain, but which many keep bottled up within them.

In spite of all the twists and turns and vagaries, in spite of touches of showmanship and exhibitionism, Buchman has never lost sight of those principles. They form the core of his philosophy. He has reiterated them through the years in varying forms and in varying settings, but always with fervour and, I believe, with complete sincerity.

What if he has seemed to stand upon his head on occasion or to play to the gallery? By extravagant devices he has probably been able to get his message through to masses of people he could never have reached otherwise. I accept that explanation. I am sure he is convinced that his ends justify any means. " And why not? " as Thackeray once asked in discussing the foibles and eccentricities of Sir Roger de Coverley. " Is the glory of Heaven to be sung only by gentlemen in black coats? Must the truth be only expounded in gown and surplice, and out of these two vestments can nobody preach it? "

After making allowances for certain absurdities, I am left in no doubt of Buchman's true teaching. I am sure he fully believes it is physically possible for everyone to " change " and come in time to the conclusion that sin of any kind doesn't pay; that life can be made worth while for everyone only when we are all agreed to abide by the rules. And the rules he propounds are honesty, purity, unselfishness, and love.

Though the argument appeals to sentiment, the very magnitude of the proposition moves most of us to dismiss it as impossible idealism. But Buchman does not say

" impossible ! " He says, in effect, " It's the only way you'll ever get a perfect world, so let's get on with it! And start with yourself. Start living the MRA way today, and tomorrow others will follow your example."

* * *

It is quite certain that a great many people do come away from Caux feeling uplifted in spirit and determined to try to lead better lives than they have done in the past. It is equally certain that a lot of those good intentions dissolve immediately sea-level is reached. But in some cases the effects are not lost. The feeling of uplift may be artificially inspired, but there is evidence that delegates have returned to their own environment to start spreading the Moral Re-Armament doctrine among others.

On this hit-and-miss principle I believe a great deal of goodwill is being disseminated. For, just as when mud is flung, some of it is bound to stick, so when ideas of virtue are scattered some of them must inevitably find their mark.

So although it is true to say that Buchman has turned Religion and Moral Uplift into Big Business, I am prepared to accept that a lot of his antics are deliberate; that he is merely giving his appeals topical twists, and putting on the kind of " shows " which he knows will attract notice.

As far back as 1938 he felt secure enough to tell a vast audience in Sweden: " I am not here to make you like me. . . ." And, a little later, in the same speech, he added: " If you are a real revolutionary, you always maintain perspective, no matter what people say about you. No matter how stones come, you go straight ahead. Stones of criticism are so bracing—they just set you up for the day."

I am satisfied that Buchman and his closest associates are deeply religious men, wholly dedicated to the titanic task they have set themselves. I respect their religious beliefs, though, as I stated at one point in my book, I am unable to share them. Where, then, do I part company? Why, if I can condone so much and can find so much to approve, am I not won over to Buchmanism?

* * *

There are numerous points on which I cannot see eye to eye with the Buchmanites.

First, there is the very keystone of all their beliefs—God-control. I have always believed in God, and I have often thought it possible for anyone to commune with the Creator and to draw comfort and strength and guidance from such communion. There is nothing mystic in this. The majority of people, I imagine, share similar thoughts.

But I cannot visualize a God who would expect His creatures to degenerate into mere puppets or to try to turn themselves into automatons or "writing mediums."

I am convinced that we are endowed with a brain so that we can work out life's problems for ourselves and learn to fight our own battles. For many years now I have carried as my watchword, these lines of Euripides:

> Try first thyself, and after call in God;
> For to the worker God Himself lends aid.

I clipped these lines from a desk calendar because they appealed to me. I quote them now because they sum up my philosophy.

But, in His wisdom, knowing our perversity, and to save us from taking too many wrong turnings, God provided us with an infallible compass—a conscience. Our success or otherwise in our progress through this world depends solely upon the use we make of that compass. When we let conscience guide us, we usually prosper; when we stifle conscience and lower our standards of right and wrong, we usually land in trouble. Most people know in their inmost hearts that this is so.

But there is another side to the " guidance " question. God, I am sure, never intended us to shuffle off all personal responsibility for our actions or to abandon personal effort. It may be very comfortable if you can convince yourself that there is no need to worry about anything any more—that God will guide and provide. But I can't accept such an easy way out. I don't believe that God will do anything for us that we are capable of doing for ourselves. It is when we are in extremity and powerless that He sometimes steps in.

*　　*　　*

This brings me to a second point in Buchmanite lore which I cannot accept. I do not like their policy where young people are concerned.

I am opposed to the regimentation of youth in any form, but religious regimentation seems to me to be most detestable of all. Of all the freedoms, freedom of worship is the most vital. Nothing but evil, I feel, can come from striving to foist ready-made ideas on young people before they are able to reason for themselves. Buchmanites may protest that they only seek to teach their young subjects to be virtuous and to respect the four absolute moral standards; but I am unmoved. They are too fond of playing upon the emotions. Consider that weeping girl at Caux.

On their own evidence it is all too clear that some adults as well as children have, as a result of these teachings, developed something akin to religious mania. This is revealed in a completely false notion of " God-control " which leads them to cite examples of " guidance " which are palpably absurd.

In a few generations the effect of such influences on susceptible people would be to produce a race of beings quite incapable of independent thought or of doing anything on their own initiative.

On this count alone I reject Buchmanism as a softening influence. It is calculated to lead impressionable youngsters and weak-minded adults to abandon all self-reliance and to accept no responsibility for their own actions. At best the habit of seeking daily " guidance " in everything can only induce a smug complacency in the practitioner who in time must shake off all sense of personal obligations and be content to " leave everything to God."

* * *

This same pernicious softening of moral fibre, it seems to me, is fostered by the unorthodox attitude of the Buchmanites towards their economic problems. As I have devoted a chapter to a factual survey of the financial side of Buchmanism, it is not necessary to add more than a few words here.

" In the sweat of thy face shalt thou eat bread," says the Bible, but some Buchmanites, ignoring this, seem to get theirs by the sweat of other people. And they don't stop at bread. They get their homes and their clothes and their cars and all the good things of life in this way.

The whole movement is supported by charitable gifts. But when I asked at headquarters whether it dispensed any charity, the reply was a frank and emphatic: " No."

No matter how sincere the followers of Buchmanism may be, no matter how zealously they may work for the cause; no matter how honest their beliefs, I cannot understand how they can possibly justify their actions simply by saying: " Where God guides, He provides."

I dislike their forced heartiness and the way in which they fawn upon the wealthy and the titled. I dislike their flattery and the way they pander to snobbish instincts. They may possibly claim that they are only exploiting human failings in others to bring people to their meetings. It still revolts me.

Finally, I think the Buchmanites have made a cardinal error in turning their energies towards high-pressure politics in general and towards anti-Communist activities in particular.

Again, they may contend that they are merely exploiting human fears of another world war to lure people to Caux to listen to the " Message." But even if that is their alibi, it still seems too drastic a departure from their registered aims of advancing the Christian religion. I think it will land them in trouble one day, for there are signs that they are creating a growing army of fanatics.

I am not surprised that some of their activities have recently brought the Movement into disfavour among the trades unions, or that prominent ecclesiastical authorities have deplored their drift away from their avowed aim of advancing the Christian religion.

But all these are purely personal views. They indicate how I feel about Buchmanism. Others think differently— among them many famous people, diplomats, politicians, scholars, and churchmen.

You, too, will decide for yourselves.

GEOFFREY WILLIAMSON

Moor Park,
   London, 1950/4

Chronology of Buchmanism

1921 Dr Buchman arrives in Oxford from China, via Cambridge.

1922 Personal evangelism among undergraduates.

1923   ,,   ,,   ,,   ,,

1924   ,,   ,,   ,,   ,,

1925   ,,   ,,   ,,   ,, Oxford and USA.

1926   ,,   ,,   ,,   ,,   ,,   ,,

1927 Holland visited.

1928 South Africa visited and first use of title " Oxford Group."

1929 South Africa re-visited.

1930 First Oxford " house-party."

1931 Oxford and South America.

1932 Canada and Oxford.

1933 Canada, and a 10,000 Assembly at Oxford.

1934 Canada and Norway, and aims proclaimed at Oxford.

1935 Norway, Denmark, New York, Oxford, Zurich.

1936 World Assembly at Birmingham. Denmark visited.

1937 Holland visited.

Note: *Up till now the movement had functioned as " A First-century Christian Fellowship," " The Oxford Group," and " Oxford Group Movement." Accent wholly on religion.*

1938 FIRST MENTION OF " MORAL RE-ARMA-MENT," East Ham. Sweden visited; and First World Assembly at Interlaken.

1939 The Oxford Group, incorporated as an Association not for profit. Dr Buchman launches MRA in America.

1940 Dr Buchman broadcasts from San Francisco.
1941 Travelling and speech-making in USA.
1942   ,,   ,,   ,,   ,,
1943   ,,   ,,   ,,   ,,
1944   ,,   ,,   ,,   ,,
1945   ,,   ,,   ,,   ,,
1946 Dr Buchman returns to London, announces post-war plans.
1947 World Assembly at Caux.
1948   ,,   ,,   ,, " Advance " in Germany.
1949   ,,   ,,   ,,
1950   ,,   ,,   ,, Second campaign in Germany.
1951 World Assembly at Mackinac Island, Michigan, USA.
1952 National Assembly at Festival Hall, London.
1953 Dr Buchman visits India with MRA team.
     The International Confederation of Free Trade Unions issues a Report deploring MRA's interference in industrial disputes.
1954 MRA becomes the centre of a prolonged press controversy and the Bishop of Colchester announces that he is personally conducting research into the Movement.
     Note: *With the introduction of " Moral Re-Armament," the Movement has tended to grow more political, and a strong anti-Communist trend has developed as the post-war campaign has gained momentum.*

Index